Wie arbeitet man am besten mit *GRAMMAR EXPLORER?*

Soll man mit Modul 1 beginnen und Modul 55 abschließen?

- Keinesfalls. Die **Module können in beliebiger Reihenfolge bearbeitet werden.**
- Im Index und den einzelnen Modulen findet man **nützliche Querverweise** auf verwandte Themen.

Dabei gilt es stets zu bedenken:
Lieber wenige Seiten konzentriert bearbeiten als viele Seiten schnell und oberflächlich.

Wozu dient die Aufgabenspalte im Rand jeder Seite?

- Sie ist das **Navigationssystem** des *Grammar Explorer*. **Es führt Lernende** sicher durch den Lernstoff **zum Ziel.**
- Es dient so lange als **Stütze, bis man den Weg** zum Verstehen **eigenständig zurücklegen kann.**

Welche Tipps sollte man bei der Arbeit an einem Modul berücksichtigen?

- Zum 'Aufwärmen' und zur Orientierung zunächst **die Augen über das gesamte Modul wandern lassen.**

  Der **Überblick** ist die **Grundlage fürs Lernen.**
- Die **Aufgaben in der Aufgabenspalte lesen** und **den jeweiligen Teil des Lernstoffes dabei betrachten.**

  Das hilft **mit dem Lernstoff vertraut** zu **werden.**

Weshalb soll man einige der Aufgaben ins eigene Übungsheft übertragen?

- Beim Übertragen füllt man nicht nur Lücken, sondern schreibt **den gesamten Sinnzusammenhang** auf.

  Das **fördert längerfristiges Behalten.**
- Es ist ratsam, jeweils den Modultitel als Überschrift einzutragen, bevor man eine Aufgabe beginnt.

Was hilft einem das Suchen von Vokabeln im Eingangstext eines Moduls?

- Die deutschen Entsprechungen helfen, einige schwierige Textstellen zu verstehen. Man braucht die Wörter nicht im Wörterbuch nachzuschlagen.
- Häufig bemerkt man bereits hier die **Unterschiede und Gemeinsamkeiten des Englischen und Deutschen.**

Was bedeuten die farbig markierten Textstellen, Überschriften von Tabellen und Listen sowie einzelne Ausdrücke und Wörter?

- Farbmarkierungen haben in all diesen Fällen eine wichtige **Hilfsfunktion**.
- Neben dem Navigationssystem sind sie **Wegweiser zur Lösung der Aufgaben**.

Wie soll man die bunten Tabellen verstehen, die sich in fast allen Modulen über Verben befinden?

- Die Tabellen zeigen, von links nach rechts, über welche **Zeit (time)** eine ***Verbform*** **(*tense*)** Auskunft gibt:

die **Vergangenheit** (mit dem ***simple past***)
die **Zeit von der Vergangenheit bis zur Gegenwart** (mit dem ***present perfect***)
die **Gegenwart** (mit dem ***present progressive*** und gelegentlich auch mit dem ***simple present***)
die **Zukunft** (mit dem ***will***- oder dem ***going to***-Futur)
die **Gegenwart und** die **Zukunft** (mit ***Modalverben***)
über **Dauerzustände und regelmäßig geschehende Dinge** (mit dem ***simple present***).

Weshalb muss man Merksätze und andere Aufgaben aus unterschiedlichen Hinweisen 'zusammenbasteln'?

- **Das hält das Gehirn auf Trab**.

Der **Fernsehmonitor** (*HINT*) gibt die grundlegende Hilfe zur Lösung der Aufgaben.
Grüne Hinweise zu Beginn eines Moduls liefern allgemeine Informationen zum Thema.
Kleine farbige Kästen, häufig auch in der Aufgabenspalte, geben unterstützende Informationen.

... und die **Lösungen** zu den Merksätzen findet man **im Anhang**.

Und wieso bekomme ich in dieser Garmmatik nichts Fertiges präsentiert?

- ... dazu ein Zitat von Konfuzius:

Sage es mir, und ich vergesse es;
Zeige es mir, und ich erinnere mich;
Lasse es mich tun, und ich behalte es.

- Notwendig sind lediglich **Stifte, ein 'großes' Heft** (Din A4) für die Aufgaben ... sowie **Ruhe und etwas Zeit**.

abbreviations

English has similar abbreviations to many other languages. You say many of them in the same way.

1. some common abbreviations

pound(s) ★ minidisc ★ gigabyte
dollar(s) ★ metre(s) ★ doctor ★ that is
Yen ★ etcetera ★ kilometres per hour
megabyte ★ degree(s) Celsius
kilogram(s) ★ Mister ★ miles per hour
Euro ★ in the morning ★ for example
['mɪsɪz] ★ centimetre(s) ★ and
disc jockey ★ in the afternoon/evening
[məz] ★ gram(s) ★ kilometre(s)
compact disc ★ degree(s) Fahrenheit
World Wide Web

°C • Mr Wills • ¥120 • & • i.e.
€1 • Mrs Jones • 40 g • 4 Gb • e.g.
9 pm • etc • 1000 m • a CD
an MD • www • Ms Webb • 40 kg
1.4 Mb • 5 am • DJ • Dr Williams
100 km • £5 • °F • 30 mph • $20
10 cm • 50 kph

titles: Mr, ______, ______, ______

weights: g, ______

measurements: cm, ______, ______

speed: kph, ______

temperatures: °C, ______

music: ______, ______, ______

money: ¥, ______, ______, ______

writing: e.g., ______, ______, ______

computers: Mb, ______, ______

time: am, ______

Abkürzungen

Bei manchen Abkürzungen im Deutschen sagst du nur die Buchstaben (*CD*), andere liest du überhaupt nicht als Abkürzung (*vier Dollar vierzig*), und wieder andere sprichst du als ein Wort aus (*DOS*).

Sieh dir das grüne Feld an, finde für jedes Wort/jeden Ausdruck die entsprechende Abkürzung in dem blauen Feld und trage diese in eine der zehn Gruppen darunter ein. (Einige Abkürzungen stehen bereits in der Tabelle.)

Übertrage die Tabelle in dein Übungsheft und füge jeweils das entsprechende Wort hinzu.

2. two exercises

Remember to pronounce 'Ms' as [məz].

find the pairs

1. Mr – Mister
   ... – ['mɪsɪz]
2. ... – kilogram
   ... – kilometre
3. ... – minidisc
   ... – compact disc
4. ... – dollar
   ... – pound
5. ... – in the morning
   ... – in the afternoon/evening
6. ... – and
   ... – for example

secret codes

[iː'dʒiː] – *e.g.*
[eɪ'em] – ...
[diː'dʒeɪ] – ...
[piː'em] – ...
[siː 'diː] – ...
[aɪ 'iː] – ...
[em'diː] – ...

Sieh dir zunächst diese beiden Übungen an. Übertrage sie in dein Übungsheft und ergänze die fehlenden Abkürzungen. (Die Abkürzungen stehen in Abschnitt 1 und die Lösung zu *secret codes* unten auf der Seite.)

3. abbreviations in a dictionary

best [best] *adv*

aunt [ɑːnt AE ænt] *n* sister of ...

she [ʃiː] *pers pron*

clean [kliːn] *adj*

enemy ['enəmi] *n* (*pl* –mies)

sing [sɪŋ] *v* (*pt* sang [sæŋ], *pp* sung [sʌŋ])

adj	verb
adv	past participle
n	past tense
pl	adverb
pp	adjective
pers pron	plural
v	noun
AE	personal pronoun
pt	American English

Hier sind einige Beispiele aus einem Wörterbuch. Ordne die Abkürzungen den Wörtern in der Liste zu. Finde mit Hilfe eines englischen Wörterbuchs heraus, für welche englischen Wörter die folgenden Abkürzungen stehen: *prep, conj, sing, BE, sb, sth, inf, phr.*

e.g., am, DJ, pm, CD, i.e., MD

Adjektive (1): Einleitung

Sieh dir das Bild, die Überschrift und den Zeitungsartikel an. Finde heraus, weshalb die Kinder neu beginnen müssen.

Suche dann die englischen Entsprechungen für 'sie scheinen glücklich zu sein', 'die gleiche Sprache wie', 'ihre Stadt ist ihnen nicht vertraut', 'Flüchtlinge', 'um vor ... zu fliehen', 'erfolgreich', 'in kurzer Zeit fließend sprechen', 'sie haben die Sprache noch nicht gelernt' und 'bis die Probleme in meiner Heimat gelöst sind'.

Im Text sind drei Adjektive markiert. Finde weitere fünfzehn und markiere sie. (Die Lösung steht unten auf der Seite.)

2 adjectives (1): introduction

Adjectives describe a person or thing, or they give information about them.

1. the position of adjectives

Starting again

Lorna and Tulani are **new** pupils in their school.

They seem **happy**, but school is **difficult** for them. They do not speak the same language as the other pupils. They have no friends. Their town is not familiar to them.

Lorna and Tulani are refugees. They have left their country to escape from war and hunger.

However, if they want to be successful, they must get a good education and they must learn the language of their new country.

"It's very difficult," says Lorna. "I go to special classes in my school. Every day I must learn 100 words. I was always an excellent pupil, but here it is not easy. I must study all my subjects in a foreign language."

Tulani says, "When you are young, you can become fluent in a short time. Life is more difficult for my parents. They haven't learnt the language here yet. I hope we can stay here until the problems in my country are over."

(Based on an article in *The Guardian*)

Sieh dir nun den unvollständigen Merksatz, den Hinweis unten sowie die Wörter vor und hinter jedem Adjektiv im Text an.

Vervollständige dann den Merksatz und übertrage ihn in dein Übungsheft.

Die meisten englischen ________________ können an zwei Stellen stehen: ____________ einem Nomen (*new pupils, the* ____________ *language, a* ____________ *education*) oder ____________ einer Form von Verben wie *be*, ____________, ______________ (*School is difficult. They seem* ___________. *You can become* ______________ *in a short time. If they want to be* ______________, *they must get* ____________________________).

Most English adjectives can go in two places:
– before a noun,
– after a form of verbs like *be, seem, become*.

2. an exercise: opposites of some common adjectives

Hier hast du zwei Gruppen von Adjektiven. Lege in deinem Übungsheft eine Tabelle an, in die du Gegensatzpaare wie *bad – good* einträgst.

bad • beautiful • boring • near
careful • cheap • clever • dangerous
difficult • dirty • early • fast • fat • full
happy • hard • high • long • noisy
true • weak • wide • warm • young

careless • clean • cold • easy • empty
exciting • expensive • false • good
late • low • far • narrow • old • quiet
sad • safe • short • slow • soft • strong
stupid • thin • ugly

same, other, familiar, successful, good, new, difficult, special, excellent, easy, foreign, young, fluent, short, difficult

3 adjectives (2): comparison of adjectives

Adjektive (2): die Steigerung von Adjektiven

1. comparative forms

Sieh dir die Überschrift und die Sprechblasen an. Finde die englischen Entsprechungen für 'ziemlich alt', 'noch älter', 'gemütlich', 'Gibt es keinen ...?' und 'teurer'.

In den Sprechblasen sind zwei Adjektive und ihre Komparativformen markiert. Finde weitere vier Beispiele und markiere sie.

Adjektive kann man mit *-er* oder *more* steigern. Die meisten kurzen Adjektive werden mit der Endung ______ gesteigert (*clean* – __________). Die meisten _______________ Adjektive (_________ oder _________ Silben) werden mit __________ gesteigert (*expensive* – __________________________).

HINT
Short adjectives:
one syllable + *-er*
Longer adjectives:
more + two or more syllables

Ergänze nun den Merksatz mithilfe des Hinweises und der markierten Formen. Übertrage den Merksatz in dein Übungsheft.

2. two-syllable adjectives with the ending *-y*

Sieh dir die Überschrift und die Sprechblasen mit Komparativformen an. Lies dann den Merksatz und den Hinweis darunter. Ergänze den Merksatz und übertrage ihn in dein Übungsheft.

_______________ Adjektive, die auf ____ enden, werden durch Anhängen von ______ gesteigert. Anstatt *-y* schreibt man ________.

More two-syllable adjectives + *-er*:
clever – cleverer
narrow – narrower
quiet – quieter
simple – simpler

HINT Kick out the *y*, punch in an *i* and add *-er*.

Sieh dir die beiden markierten Superlativformen an. Finde zwei weitere und markiere sie.

Ergänze dann den Merksatz mithilfe des Hinweises und übertrage ihn in dein Übungsheft.

HINT

comparative form	superlative form
☺	☺
...-er	→ ...-est
more ...	→ most ...

Lies die zwei Sprechblasen und den Hinweis.

HINT

If an adjective ends with -e, add -r and -st.
And for hot, big, fat ... ? You double the consonant.
Got that?

Lege in deinem Übungsheft zwei Tabellen an – wie im Beispiel rechts – und trage die Steigerungsformen der Adjektive aus den Wolken ein.

Sieh dir diese Adjektivformen an und ergänze die Formen rechts mit den Formen aus der Wolke.

Blättere zurück zu den Adjektiven auf Seite 6 unten. Ordne sie je einer der vier Gruppen rechts zu – zuerst auf einem Notizblatt, dann in deinem Übungsheft.

3. superlative forms

Adjektive, die ihre Komparativform mit *-er* bilden, haben die

Endung ____________ für ihre ______________________________________.

Adjektive, die für ihre ______________________________ *more* benötigen,

bilden ihre ______________________ mit ___________.

4. a note about the spelling of some comparative and superlative forms

fine – free
large – late – nice – safe
simple – true – white

big – fat
hot – sad
thin – wet

strange – stranger – strangest
... – ...

mad – madder – maddest
...

5. some special comparative and superlative forms

worse more
best most
more further

good, better, ____________

much, __________, __________

far, __________, *furthest*

bad, __________, *worst*

many, __________, *most*

6. an exercise

one-syllable adjectives (*-er/-est*)

adjectives with a special comparative and superlative form

two-syllable adjectives ending in *-y* and some other adjectives (*-er/-est*)

adjectives with two or more syllables (*more/most*)

4 adjectives (3): comparisons in sentences

Dear James,
You wanted to know how ***good*** *our sports teams are this year. We have been very* ***successful*** *in our matches against the other schools.*
This year our basketball team is ***as successful as*** *King Edward's, and it's* ***better than*** *St Luke's.*
Our football team has not been as successful as our basketball team. The team is not as good as last year.
Our hockey team is as good as ever. We have been more successful than St Luke's and King Edward's.
Our swimming team is the most successful team in the school. I think we are even better than last year. Perhaps our team is the best we have ever had. We are twice as successful as St Luke's and ten times better than King Edward's.
And can you believe it? Yesterday Jessica said nobody on the swimming team is better than me.
Write soon – the sooner the better.
Neal

School sports

FOOTBALL
5th King Edward's School
6th St Luke's School
7th Park School

BASKETBALL
3rd King Edward's School
3rd Park School
4th St Luke's School

HOCKEY
2nd Park School
3rd St Luke's School
4th King Edward's School

SWIMMING
1st Park School
3rd St Luke's School
7th King Edward's School

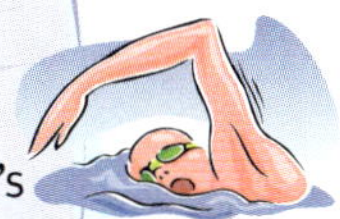

successful
as … – …
not as … – …
more successful than – …
the most successful – …
twice …

good
better than – …
not as good as – …
as … ever – …
even … – …
… ever had – …
ten … – …
… me – …
the … – …

an exercise: puzzle it out

- *der/die/das beste*
- *doppelt so gut wie*
- *noch erfolgreicher als*
- *erfolgreicher als ich*
- *der/die/das erfolgreichste, den/die/das wir je hatten*
- *zehnmal erfolgreicher als*

And what is "*Je erfolgreicher, desto besser*" in English?

Adjektive (3): Vergleiche in Sätzen

Sieh dir die Überschrift, die vier Tabellen mit verschiedenen Mannschaften und den Brief an.
Finde heraus, in welche Schule Neal geht und welchen Sport er treibt.

In dem Brief sind die Adjektive *good* und *successful* sowie zwei Vergleiche markiert.
Finde insgesamt elf weitere Ausdrücke zum Vergleichen und markiere sie.

Lege dir dann in deinem Übungsheft zwei Listen an, wie die Beispiele unter dem Brief.
Ordne den englischen Ausdrücken jeweils die Entsprechungen aus den beiden deutschen Listen zu.

besser als – je früher, desto besser – so gut wie immer – besser als ich – noch besser als – der/die/das beste, den/die/das wir je hatten – nicht so gut wie – zehnmal besser als

erfolgreicher als – doppelt so erfolgreich wie – so erfolgreich wie – der/die/das erfolgreichste – nicht so erfolgreich wie

Sieh dir diese Ausdrücke zum Vergleichen an.
Mit Hilfe der Ausdrücke aus dem Brief kannst du sie ins Englische übertragen und deinen beiden Listen hinzufügen.

5 adverbials

Adverbiale

Lies den Dialog und finde heraus, weshalb Lisa in die USA fliegt.

Suche dann die englischen Entsprechungen für ‘ich bin nicht zurück am Wochenende’, ‘ich war noch nie in den USA’, ‘du wirst viel Spaß haben’ und ‘leider’.

In dem Dialog sind je zwei Adverbiale der Zeit und des Ortes markiert. Finde weitere dreizehn und markiere sie. (Die Lösung steht unten auf der Seite.)

An *adverbial* is a group of words that can tell you *where* (= adverbial of place) or *when* (= adverbial of time) something happens or is done.

1. types of adverbials

Lisa, why can’t you come to my Halloween party **next Saturday**?

I’m flying **to California**. Didn’t I tell you, Vanessa? I’m leaving on Wednesday. I won’t be back at the weekend. I’ve never been **in the USA on October 31st.**

You’ll have a nice time. Two years ago I stayed at my sister’s house in my autumn holidays. She lives near Washington DC, in a small town in Maryland. I was also in New York for a few days. In New York I stayed in a super hotel. Unfortunately, I had to fly back a few days before Halloween.

October 31st, Halloween

Übertrage die *adverbials* in zwei Listen in dein Übungsheft – wie in den Beispielen.

adverbials of place
to California
in the …

adverbials of time
next Saturday
on …

These adverbials normally go at the end of a sentence. The adverbial of place usually comes before the adverbial of time.

HINT

2. the position of adverbials

Sieh dir den Merksatz, die Hinweise und die Stellung der *adverbials* im Dialog an. Vervollständige dann den Merksatz und übertrage ihn zusammen mit dem Hinweis in dieser Spalte in dein Übungsheft.

Adverbiale des Ortes und der ______________ stehen gewöhnlich am ______________ eines Satzes. Das Adverbial des ______________ kommt vor dem Adverbial der ______________ (*p before t*). Wenn der Ort oder die ______________ wichtig sind, können diese Adverbiale auch am ______________ des Satzes stehen.

Be careful:
I was in New York for two days.
Ich war zwei Tage in New York.

3. some useful adverbials of time to talk about …

Useful expressions

Übertrage diese *adverbials of time* in Form von *spidergrams* in dein Übungsheft.

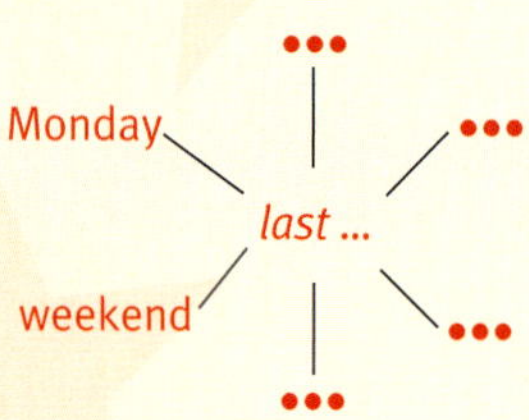

the past: last Monday, ~ week, ~ month, ~ year, …
a minute ago, half an hour ~, an hour ~, three days ~, a week ~, …
yesterday morning, ~ afternoon, ~evening
last night, ~ Sunday morning, …; the day before yesterday

the past and the future:
this morning, ~ afternoon, ~ evening, ~ week, ~ month, ~ year, …
today, tonight, on Saturday, at the weekend

the future: next Monday, ~ week, …
in a minute, ~ half an hour, …
tomorrow morning, ~ afternoon, ~ night, …
next Sunday morning, the day after tomorrow

on Wednesday, at the weekend, two years ago, at my sister’s house, in my autumn holidays, near Washington DC, in a small town, in Maryland, in New York, for a few days, in New York, in a super hotel, a few days before Halloween

6 adverbs (1): introduction

Adverbien (1): Einleitung

1. types of adverbs

Adverbs are single words.
They tell you:
- *how* (adverbs of manner),
- *where* (adverbs of place),
- *when* (adverbs of time),
- *how often* (adverbs of frequency)

something happens or is done.

Around 1600, English Catholics had a hard time. King James I did not let Catholics pray freely.
In November 1605 some Catholics (a man called Guy Fawkes and his friends) decided to blow up the Houses of Parliament in London.
They hoped to blow up King James, too.

Sieh dir das Bild, die Überschrift und den Text an. Finde heraus, weshalb am 5. November überall in England Freudenfeuer angezündet werden.

Suche die englischen Entsprechungen für 'um 1600', 'ein Mann, der ... hieß', 'sie durchsuchen oft ...', 'wir müssen uns immer heimlich treffen', 'wir können nicht offen sprechen', 'sie wurden hingerichtet', 'zum ersten Mal' und 'sogar heute noch'.

My friends and I often talk about our plan.
We have thought about everything carefully.
I found a safe place for our gunpowder yesterday.
Nobody will find it there.
Here the King's men might find it today.
They often search the houses of Catholics.
Tonight I will go and speak to my friends.
We must always meet secretly.
We can't speak openly everywhere.
I hope we can complete the first part of our plan successfully tomorrow.

November 5th, Bonfire Night

Guy Fawkes and his friends were not successful. They were caught and executed. On November 5th, 1606, people celebrated this execution for the first time. They made a big fire, called a bonfire, and burnt a straw doll, 'a guy', on it. Even today people celebrate 'Guy Fawkes Day' on November 5th with fireworks and bonfires on which they burn 'a guy'.

In der Sprechblase siehst du vier unterschiedlich markierte Adverbien:
- Adverbien der Art und Weise
- Ortsadverbien
- Zeitadverbien
- Häufigkeitsadverbien.

Finde insgesamt zehn weitere Adverbien in der Sprechblase und markiere sie. (Die Lösung steht unten auf der Seite.)

adverbs of manner
(How?)
carefully
...

adverbs of place
(Where?)
there
...

adverbs of time
(When?)
...

adverbs of frequency
(How often?)
...

Lege dir dann in deinem Übungsheft vier Tabellen an und übertrage alle Adverbien aus der Sprechblase.

2. an exercise: Bonfire Night

________________ the children made 'a guy' for our bonfire in the back garden.

Are you going to have a bonfire ________________, too?

– No, there'll be bonfires ________________ in our street. Do you ________________ have your bonfire in the back garden?

No, ________________ we have it in the front garden.

– Be careful. Bonfires can get out of control very ________________.

sometimes
quickly
everywhere
yesterday
usually
tonight

Sieh dir den unvollständigen Dialog und die sechs Adverbien an.
Trage dann die Adverbien so ein, dass sich ein sinnvoller Dialog ergibt. (Die Lösung steht unten auf der Seite.)

adverbs: here, today, often, tonight, always, secretly, openly, everywhere, successfully, tomorrow // **exercise:** yesterday, tonight, everywhere, usually, sometimes, quickly

Sieh dir die Tagebucheinträge an und finde heraus, weshalb Guy Fawkes seinen Freunden Mut zusprechen musste.

Finde die englischen Entsprechungen für 'wir haben dort unseren Sprengstoff versteckt', 'die Leute des Königs werden ihn niemals finden', '(sie) werden morgen überall sein', 'wir könnten uns dann hier nicht sicher verstecken' und 'ich sage ihnen immer …'.

Im Text sind fünf Adverbien markiert. Finde weitere zehn und markiere sie. (Die Lösung steht unten auf der Seite.)

3. the position of adverbs (in general)

From the diary of Guy Fawkes

My friends and I will meet **tonight.** **Tomorrow** King James will open Parliament. We have hidden our gunpowder **there.** The King's men will **never** find it.

We have planned everything **perfectly.** We can blow up Parliament easily.

The King's men will be everywhere tomorrow. We must leave quickly tonight. We couldn't hide safely here then.

My friends are sometimes frightened. I always tell them that we will succeed.

HINT

Adverbs of manner, of place and of time are normally in end-position.
Adverbs of time can also be in front-position.
Adverbs of frequency are normally in mid-position.

Sieh dir nun den unvollständigen Merksatz, die Hinweise und den Text an.

Remember:
When there is more than one adverb in end-position, *manner comes before place and before time.*

Ergänze den Merksatz und übertrage ihn in dein Übungsheft.

! Adverbien können an ___________ Stellen stehen:
am Satzanfang, mitten im Satz und am _______________.
Adverbien der _____________________, Ortsadverbien und
Zeitadverbien stehen gewöhnlich am _______________.
Bei mehreren Adverbien am _______________ gilt die Regel:
"_______________ comes before _____________ and before _______________."
Zeitadverbien können auch am _________________ stehen.
Häufigkeitsadverbien stehen gewöhnlich _____________ im Satz.

4. the position of adverbs of frequency (details)

Lies den zweiten Merksatz, den Hinweis rechts und noch einmal den Text oben. Vervollständige dann den Merksatz und übertrage ihn in dein Übungsheft.

HINT

Adverbs of frequency go
- before a full verb
- after a form of *be*
- after the first auxiliary if the verb has more than one part.

! Besteht das Prädikat …

- nur aus einem Vollverb, steht das Häufigkeitsadverb (*adverb* _______________) _______ dem Prädikat:
  I always ______________________________.
- nur aus einer Form von *be*, steht es _____________ der Form von *be*:
  My friends ______________________________.
- aus mehr als einem Teil, steht es ____________ dem ersten Hilfsverb:
  The King's men ______________________________.

some adverbs of frequency:

always	*regularly*
nearly always	*sometimes*
often	*rarely*
usually	*hardly ever*
normally	*never*

easily, everywhere, tomorrow, quickly, tonight, safely, here, then, sometimes, always

7 adverbs (2): adverbs of manner

1. the position of adverbs of manner (details)

Work through 6 *adverbs (1)* before you start here.

Adverbien (2): Adverbien der Art und Weise

Sieh dir das Bild und den Text an und finde heraus, weshalb Delfine ganz besondere Tiere sind.

Finde die englischen Entsprechungen für 'dort haben einige Delfine im Spiel Kontakt mit Menschen aufgenommen', '(sie) haben Leute bereitwillig gerettet', '..., der taub war und nicht richtig sprechen konnte', 'die Leute waren erstaunt, als ...', und 'Menschen, die furchtbar unter ... leiden'.

Im Text sind drei Prädikate mit Adverbien markiert. Finde weitere zehn Verben mit *adverbs of manner* und markiere sie. (Die Lösung steht unten auf der Seite.)

Very special animals

Dolphins **swim freely** in the world's oceans. There, some dolphins **have playfully contacted** people or have willingly rescued people. In dangerous situations they **have helped** people **quickly** and unselfishly. Such contacts can change a person's life radically.

One special dolphin lives happily in Mezina Bay on the Sinai coast in the Red Sea.

One day, she unexpectedly made contact with a fisherman who was deaf and couldn't speak properly. He had few friends, so he gladly accepted the dolphin's friendship. People were amazed when the fisherman slowly learned to speak properly. People now come from all over the world to swim with this dolphin. Sometimes she lets swimmers touch her gently. People who suffer terribly from depression often feel a new happiness after this experience.

HINT

Adverbs of manner are usually in end-position:
They swim freely in the world's oceans. / They have helped people quickly.
They can sometimes also be in mid-position:
He gladly accepted this friendship. / They have playfully contacted people.
When the verb is only one full verb, the adverb of manner goes before the full verb.
When the verb has two or more parts, the adverb of manner goes after the first auxiliary.

!

Adverbien der Art und Weise stehen gewöhnlich am ______________.

__________________ können sie auch mitten im __________ stehen.

Besteht das Prädikat aus ___________ Teil, kommt das

_____________ der Art und Weise _________ das Prädikat.

Besteht das Prädikat aus _______________________ Teilen, steht das Adverb der Art und Weise ____________ dem ersten Hilfsverb.

Vervollständige nun den Merksatz mithilfe des Hinweises darüber und der markierten Formen im Text. Übertrage ihn und die Beispielsätze aus dem Hinweis in dein Übungsheft.

2. the formation of adverbs of manner

speak clearly • rain heavily
play terribly • write (a letter) neatly
discuss a problem sensibly
spell a word correctly • walk funnily
explain a rule simply • work happily
look nastily at somebody
smile nervously • think carefully about
leave (the office) quickly

HINT

- Almost all adverbs of manner are formed with an adjective + *-ly*.
- Almost all adjectives which end with *-y* (*happy*) change this to an *-i* (*happily*).
- Some adjectives which end with *-e* (*comfortable*) drop this letter (*comfortably*).
- These three adverbs don't end in *-ly*: *well, hard, fast*.

Sieh dir den Kasten, die drei Tabellen und den Hinweis an.

Lege in deinem Übungsheft drei solche Tabellen an. Ordne die *verbs + adverbs* der jeweiligen Tabelle zu. Füge die *verbs + adverbs* aus dem Text oben hinzu.

adjective + *ly*
speak clearly
…

adjective(y>i) + *ly*
rain heavily
…

adjective(~~e~~) + y
play terribly
…

have willingly rescued, change … radically, lives happily, unexpectedly made contact, speak properly, gladly accepted, slowly learned, speak properly, touch … gently, suffer terribly

In diesem Text erfährst du mehr über den besonderen Delfin.

Finde die englischen Entsprechungen für 'er war selbstbewusster als ...', 'er konnte sich leicht verständigen mit ...' und '(sie) sprechen am begeistertsten über ...'.

3. the comparison of adverbs of manner

When the dolphin came to the bay, everybody in the village **spoke excitedly about her**.

Soon people saw a change in the fisherman: He **behaved more self-confidently than** before. He learned to **speak as clearly as** they did. And he could **communicate easily with** them.

Of course, the people who come to swim in the bay **speak most excitedly about** the dolphin. Some feel they can **communicate most easily with** the dolphin, **more easily than** with any human being.

HINT

For the ...
- comparative form you use *more + adverb of manner*
- superlative form you use *most + adverb of manner.*

Vervollständige nun die Tabelle mit Steigerungsformen mithilfe des Hinweises rechts. Übertrage die Tabelle und die beiden Hinweise in dein Übungsheft.

adverb →	comparative form →	superlative form
easily,	*more easily (than),*	*most easily*
excitedly,	______,	*most excitedly*
______,	*more self-confidently (than),*	______
(as) clearly (as),	______,	______

These **adverbs of manner** don't need *more* or *most*:
well, better, best
badly, worse, worst
fast, faster, fastest
hard, harder, hardest

4. adjective or adverb: a problem for you?

Sieh dir diese Sätze an und vervollständige sie.

Markiere die deutschen Entsprechungen für die Adjektive *peaceful* und *good* sowie die Adverbien *peacefully* und *well*.

Mezina Bay **is peaceful.**

Mezina Bay ist friedlich.

The dolphin **lives peacefully** in the bay.

Der Delfin ______ *in der Bucht.*

The fisherman and the dolphin are **good friends.**

Der Fischer ______ ______.

They **know** each other **well.**

Sie kennen ______.

Welchen Fehler, denkst du, machen Lernende häufig, wenn sie *adverbs of manner* verwenden sollten?

5. an exercise: adjective or adverb?

Sieh dir diesen unvollständigen Text und die Adjektive und Adverbien in der Wolke an.

Übertrage dann den Text in dein Übungsheft und ergänze die Adjektive und Adverbien sinnvoll. (Eine Lösung steht unter dem Text.)

strong – well
intelligent – big
aggressive – ~~safely~~
heavy – closely – easily
faster – intelligently
hard – lovingly
important – better

Some more about dolphins

In the oceans dolphins live *safely* in groups that have a … leader. Experts have found out that physical contact is very … for dolphins. They often swim … together, touch each other … with their flippers and 'talk' to each other. However, no dictionary of 'Dolphinese' exists.

At birth, the brain of a dolphin is about as … as a baby's brain. It develops … than the human brain. When a dolphin is nine years old, its brain is as … as a 17-year-old human's brain: about 1,400 to 1,500 g.

Dolphins are possibly the most … animals. In experiments they behave much more … than chimps and they understand things ….

Life in isolation is … for dolphins. They hardly ever behave as … as in groups. They can be quite …. They even stop eating and … become ill or even die.

Be careful:
Life **is hard.** = It is not easy.
She **works hard.** = She works a lot.
They **hardly ever** behave well. = They **don't often** behave well.

strong, important, closely, lovingly, big, faster, heavy, intelligent, intelligently, better, hard, well, aggressive, easily

8 the alphabet

1. the letters of the alphabet

Knowing the alphabet will help you to write what another person spells. It will also help you to spell your name, place names or difficult words for other people.

das Alphabet

Sieh dir die Buchstaben und die Lautschrift dazu an. Übe dann, das Alphabet in unterschiedlicher Reihenfolge laut zu lesen: vorwärts, rückwärts, nach Spalten usw.

a [eɪ]	b [bi:]	c [si:]		
d [di:]	e [i:]	f [ef]	g [dʒi:]	h [eɪtʃ]
i [aɪ]	j [dʒeɪ]	k [keɪ]	l [el]	m [em]
n [en]	o [əʊ]	p [pi:]	q [kju:]	r [ɑ:]
s [es]	t [ti:]	u [ju:]	v [vi:]	w ['dʌblju:]
x [eks]	y [waɪ]	z *BE* [zed] *US* [zi:]		

HINT

- The five **red letters** letters are **vowels**.
- The twenty-one **black letters** are **consonants**.
- Most English words start with a small letter.
- You use **CAPITAL LETTERS** for the beginning of a sentence, for all names (*Mike*, *Wales*, *Sunday*), nationalities (*British*), languages (*English*) and the personal pronoun *I*.
- When two letters are together and they are the same (*-tt-*), you say *double (t)*.

The German letters *ä*, *ö*, *ü* are *a-/o-/u-Umlaut*. You say [ˌeɪ'ʊmlaʊt], ... The German letter *ß* is *double s* in English.

Das ________________ hat 26 Buchstaben, ______ Vokale (*a*, _____, _____, _____, _____) und _______ Konsonanten (*b*, *c*, etc). Die _______________ englischen Wörter beginnen mit Kleinbuchstaben. Du verwendest _________________________ nur am ________________ des Satzes, für alle ________________, Nationalitäten, ____________________ und für das Personalpronomen _______. Für Doppelbuchstaben (*-tt-*) sagt man *double (t)*.

Lies den unvollständigen Merksatz und den Hinweis. Ergänze dann den Merksatz und übertrage ihn zusammen mit dem Hinweis oben in dein Übungsheft.

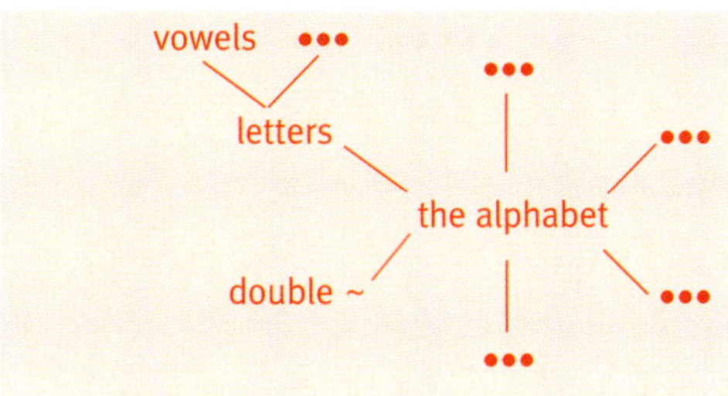

5, 21
capital letters
small letters
nationalities
languages
names

Lege in deinem Übungsheft ein kleines *spidergram* mit wichtigen Wörtern zum Thema *the alphabet* an.

Sieh dir diese unvollständigen Sätze und die Wörter rechts oben an. Vervollständige dann die Sätze. (Die Lösung steht unten auf der Seite.) Übertrage die Sätze in dein Übungsheft.

2. an exercise: some phrases for spelling

is – spell – at – sorry – to – spell – double – spell – a – spelt

1. I'm __________, I didn't get that. Could you ________ it more slowly?
2. How do you ___________ it, with one 's' or with '___________-s'?
3. I think it _______ spelt as two words, not one.
4. There is _____ 'w' missing ______ the end of the word.
5. 'Lovely' is ____________ with an 'e' after the 'v'.
6. I'm not sure how ________ spell that word.
7. Do you ____________ it with an 'i' or a 'y'?

3. the international phonetic alphabet

Lies den Hinweis und sieh dir das Bild und das *International Phonetic Alphabet* an.

Übe dann, die Wörter in der Wolke, deinen Namen und deine Adresse mithilfe dieses Alphabets zu buchstabieren.

Can you spell that for me, please?

Pachtschenko, p as in Papa, Alpha, Charlie, Hotel…

For international communication it can be important to know the phonetic alphabet. When you have to spell the names of people or places, this will help to avoid mistakes.

This is just one of several 'phonetic alphabets' that people use in the English-speaking world. Sometimes people make up their own alphabet with names of people and places.

a	–	Alpha	j	–	Juliet	s	–	Sierra
b	–	Bravo	k	–	Kilo	t	–	Tango
c	–	Charlie	l	–	Lima	u	–	Uniform
d	–	Delta	m	–	Mike	v	–	Victor
e	–	Echo	n	–	November	w	–	Whisky
f	–	Foxtrot	o	–	Oscar	x	–	X-ray
g	–	Golf	p	–	Papa	y	–	Yankee
h	–	Hotel	q	–	Quebec	z	–	Zulu
i	–	India	r	–	Romeo			

Lyudmila – Betelgeuse – Ystad – Beerenbrouck – Kyzyl Kum – Schweikert – Kangchenjunga

4. some punctuation marks

Hier hast du die englischen Wörter für die wichtigsten Satzzeichen. Übertrage sie in dein Übungsheft.

.	full stop	/	slash
?	question mark	( )	brackets
!	exclamation mark	[ ]	square brackets
,	comma	'	apostrophe
:	colon	'…'	(single) quotation marks
;	semi-colon	"…"	(double) quotation marks
-	hyphen		
–	dash		

1. Sorry / spell; 2. spell / double; 3. is; 4. a / at; 5. spelt; 6. to; 7. spell

9 articles (1): definite and indefinite

Artikel (1): der bestimmte und der unbestimmte Artikel

1. the definite article (*the*)

The English language has three articles (*the, a, an*). Their form never changes.

Sieh dir das Bild und den Text an und finde heraus, wie der Buchstabe *X* zum Zeichen für einen Kuss wurde.

Finde dann die englischen Entsprechungen für 'die Englisch sprechende Welt', 'an diesem Tag', 'die Leute, die sie mögen oder lieben', 'vor langer Zeit', 'sie unterzeichneten Dokumente mit einem Kreuz', 'sie hatten die Wahrheit gesagt', 'das Kreuz', 'die andere Erklärung' und 'der griechische Buchstabe'.

Valentine's Day – February 14th

Post offices in **the English-speaking world** – and in many other countries – are very busy on 14 February. On that day, lots of people send cards to **the people** they like or love. At **the end** of these 'Valentine cards' they often write *"xxx"*.

Today everybody sees **the letter *"x"*** as a symbol for a kiss. A long time ago **the sign *"X"*** under a document was really a cross, not a letter from **the alphabet.**

When people couldn't write their name, they put a cross under documents. To show that they had told **the truth,** they kissed **the document.**

There are two explanations for **the cross.** Some people say it is **the cross** of St. Andrew. **The other explanation** is that it is **the Greek letter** 'Chi', a short form for the name 'Christ'.

Im Deutschen gibt es ____________ bestimmte

_____________________ (*der, die, das*).

Im Englischen gibt es nur _____________ bestimmten

Artikel (_________________*article*): ___________.

In den _____________ Fällen wird __________ als [ðə] ausgesprochen.

Nur wenn der erste ____________ des folgenden Wortes ein _____________ ist,

sagt man [ði].

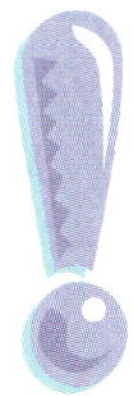

Vervollständige nun diesen Merksatz. Die drei Hinweise und die markierten Teile im Text helfen dir dabei.
Übertrage den Merksatz und den Hinweis in dieser Spalte in dein Übungsheft.

- There is only one definite article in English: *the*.
- *The* is pronounced in two ways: [ðə] or [ði].
- In most cases it is pronounced [ðə].
- When the first sound of the following word is a vowel, you say [ði].

Remember:

English	German
letter	*Buchstabe*
sound	*Laut*
vowel	*Vokal*
consonant	*Konsonant*

2. an exercise

Sieh dir nun die Wörter links und die Tabelle an.
Ordne die Wörter der jeweiligen Spalte zu und trage sie in der vorgegebenen Reihenfolge ein.
(Die ersten Buchstaben der **Nomen** in jeder Spalte ergeben jeweils ein dir bekanntes Wort.)

~~car~~
right ~~order~~
old ~~van~~
notes
exact opposite
other way
station
last owner
nurse
unhappy ending
wrong answer
angry lion
newspaper
new timetable

[ðə]	[ði]
car	*old van*
right order	

Lies, was der Moderator sagte, und finde heraus, was genau Lucy und Ben gewonnen haben.

Finde die englischen Entprechungen für 'ein großartiger Preis', 'ein absolut sagenhafter Preis', 'eine Gelegenheit zum Einkaufen bis zum Abwinken', 'das wird ein unvergessliches Erlebnis für euch', 'weniger als eine halbe Stunde entfernt von ...' und 'schließlich ein nützlicher Tipp'.

Im Text ist je ein Ausdruck mit *a* und *an* markiert. Finde je fünf weitere Beispiele und markiere sie.

Sieh dir die beiden Hinweise und den unvollständigen Merksatz an. Vervollständige dann den Merksatz und übertrage ihn zusammen mit dem Hinweis rechts in dein Übungsheft.

3. the indefinite articles *a* and *an*

Lucy and Ben, you have won **a great prize**. No, let me say that again. You have won **an absolutely fabulous prize**.

Have you ever spent a weekend in Hong Kong? Well, you will spend an exciting weekend there. You will stay in a luxury suite in an international hotel. You will have an opportunity to shop till you drop. Why? Because we will give you $5,000 to spend. Isn't that a great opportunity? It will be a wonderful experience; it will be an unforgettable experience for you.

You will stay in a hotel that is less than half an hour from the great Tsim Sha Tsui shopping centres!

And finally a useful tip: Visit *The Hong Kong Story* in the *Museum of History*. There you can inform yourselves about Hong Kong's history in just one afternoon.

Im Englischen gibt es ________ unbestimmte Artikel (______________ *articles*): ______ und ________.

In den ____________________ benutzt man ______.

Nur wenn der erste __________ des folgenden Wortes ein __________ ist, sagt man ________.

Be careful:

[h]	a hotel	[aʊ]	an hour
[n]	a name	[en]	an 'n'
[ju:]	a unit	[ʌ]	an uncle

- English has two indefinite articles: *a* and *an*.
- In most cases you use *a*.
- Only when the first sound of the following word is a vowel sound, you use *an*.

4. an exercise

Ordne die Wörter rechts der jeweils richtigen Spalte der Tabelle zu. (Die ersten Buchstaben der **Nomen** in jeder Spalte ergeben zusammen ein dir bekanntes Wort.)

a	*an*
a nice idea	*an area*
a noise	

~~nice idea~~
~~noise~~
~~area~~
desk
angry reporter
different expression
old telephone
friend
island
young interviewer
number
expensive cake
easy lesson
big island
telephone
example
good example

10 articles (2): some special rules

einige Sonderregeln

1. with or without *the* in your language?

Where can we go for lunch? ★ Let's go by car. ★ Tim is at school.
They arrived by bus. ★ Ann is practising the violin. ★ He is still at work.
She returned from work at five. ★ It's time to go to school.
I can play the guitar. ★ Sue is in hospital. ★ Lisa is learning the trumpet.
Michael went to university last year. ★ I often eat fruit for breakfast.
Let's leave after breakfast. ★ Two of the gangsters are still in prison.
One of them escaped from prison. ★ Dinner was good. ★ I went by bike.

Sieh dir diese Sätze an und finde die englischen Entsprechungen für 'sie sind mit dem Bus angekommen', 'sie übt Geige', 'sie ist von der Arbeit zurückgekommen', 'Obst zum Frühstück essen' und 'einer ist aus dem Gefängnis geflohen'.

Übertrage die einzelnen Sätze ins Deutsche. Welche Unterschiede zwischen dem Englischen und dem Deutschen bei der Verwendung des bestimmten Artikels erkennst du?

Lege in deinem Übungsheft ein *spidergram* an, in das du die Sätze in vier Gruppen einträgst, wie in dem Beispiel links. Kennzeichne dabei die Unterschiede zum Deutschen farblich.

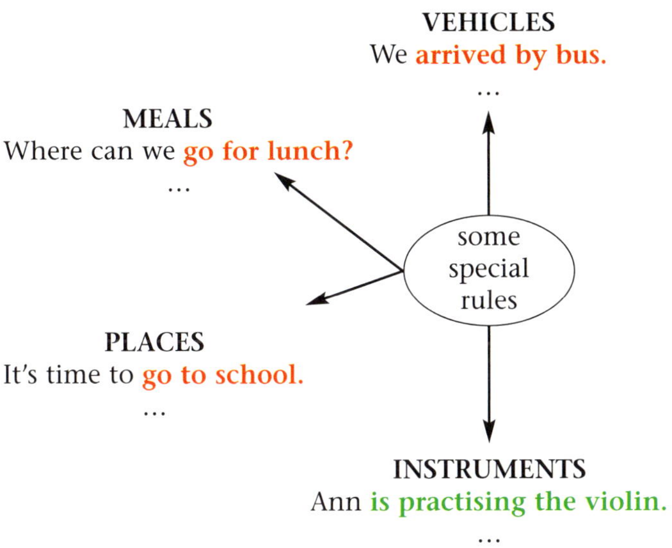

You do not use a definite article
- before the names of meals
- between a preposition and nouns like *school*, ...
- after the preposition *by* and nouns like *car*, *bus*, ...

2. with or without *a/an* in your language?

My mother is a doctor.	Luke has a sore throat.
Josh has a headache.	Susan is a pilot.
Frank is a manager.	Lisa has a high fever.
Peter has a temperature.	Amanda is a policewoman.

talking about illnesses
Luke has a sore throat.
...

talking about jobs
My mother is a doctor.
...

Sieh dir diese Sätze an und übertrage sie ins Deutsche. Welche Unterschiede bei der Verwendung des unbestimmten Artikels kannst du feststellen?

Lege in deinem Übungsheft zwei Tabellen an und trage die Sätze ein.

Lege dir zusätzlich in deinem Übungsheft ein *spidergram* zum Thema *jobs* an.

3. some useful phrases

1. We are in a hurry.
2. We waited for a long time, but nothing happened.
3. It costs more than a hundred pounds. I can't afford that.
4. Don't make a noise. The children are asleep already.
5. It's a pity she is not here.
6. He definitely drove more than fifty kilometres an hour.

a. *Es kostet mehr als einhundert Pfund. Das kann ich mir nicht leisten.*
b. *Sei(d) bitte leise. Die Kinder schlafen schon.*
c. *Wir haben es eilig.*
d. *Wir haben lange gewartet, aber nichts passierte.*
e. *Er ist sicherlich mehr als fünfzig Stundenkilometer gefahren.*
f. *Es ist schade, dass sie nicht hier ist.*

Ordne die englischen und deutschen Sätze einander zu.

das Verb *be* (sein)

Sieh dir das Bild und die Sprechblasen an. Finde heraus, weshalb es sich um eine ungewöhnliche Familie handelt.

Finde die englischen Entsprechungen für 'du bist der zweite Pudel', 'sie ist eine gute Freundin für dich', 'verschiedene Hunderassen', 'Promenadenmischungen', 'ihr habt jetzt nichts zu tun', 'beeilt euch', 'kommt nicht zu spät' und 'zwei Welpen'.

Im Text sind zwei Personalpronomen mit Präsensformen von *be* markiert. Finde im Text die Formen, die zu *she, he, it, we, you* sowie *they* gehören und markiere sie.

Positive statements are *bejahte Aussagesätze* and negative statements are *verneinte Aussagesätze*.

Sieh dir nun die drei unvollständigen Tabellen und die Hinweise an. Übertrage die Tabellen in dein Übungsheft und ergänze sie.

For more about the short forms of *be*, see *22 long forms/ short forms*.

Lies diese Sätze und noch einmal den Text oben. Übertrage dann die Sätze in dein Übungsheft und ergänze sie mit der richtigen Form aus der Wolke. (Die Lösung steht unter den Sätzen.)

11 be

Be is the most often used verb in English.

1. talking about the present

A family with a difference

Hello, Elmo. Welcome to your new home. Are you surprised to be here? **I am Sue,** the mother of this family. **You are** the second poodle in our family.
This is Katie. She is a good friend for you. She often brings dogs without a home to us.
And that is Billy. He is the 'father' in our family. It is not always easy to live with him. He is very strict.
We are a family with many different breeds of dogs and with mongrels, too.

Bonzo and Bingo, you are free now. Please show Elmo where he can sleep. But please be quick and don't be late for lunch. You must be at your feeding bowls at 12 o'clock. Billy will be angry if you are not there.

Elmo, these two puppies are our youngest dogs. They are only two months old.

forms of *be*

positive statements		negative statements		questions	
I am	ich bin	I'm not	ich bin nicht	am I …?	Yes, you are. No, you aren't.
you are	du bist	you aren't	du bist nicht	are you …?	Yes, I am. No, I'm not.
she …	sie …	she isn't	sie …	… she …?	Yes, she is. No, she isn't.
he …	…	…	…	…	…
it …	…	…	…		
we …	…				
you …	…				
they …	…				

- When people speak, they often use short forms of *be*. When you write short forms, you must use an apostrophe (') to show that a letter is missing: *I'm, you're, she's, …*
- You make negative statements with *not (I'm not) or …n't (you aren't)* after the form of *be*.
- To make a question, put the form of *be* before the subject: *…am I, … are you, … is she …?*
  You use long forms for positive short answers: *Yes, I am; yes, you are; yes, she is, …*

2. an exercise

is – are – is – isn't – is – are – aren't – is – are – aren't – are

1. Sue … a retriever. She … the mother of the family.
2. Look at those two dogs there. They … mongrels.
3. Old Billy … quite difficult.
4. Elmo … the only poodle in the family.
5. Bonzo and Bingo … very old. They … puppies.
6. The family members … from one breed of dogs only.
7. How old … these puppies?
8. How old … Sue?
9. Where … the feeding bowls?

1. is, is; 2. are; 3. is; 4. isn't; 5. aren't, are; 6. aren't; 7. are; 8. is; 9. are

3. talking about the past and the future: positive statements

Lies dir diesen Merkvers leise vor und finde heraus, weshalb die Formen leicht zu behalten sind.

Finde die englischen Entsprechungen für 'es ist einfach ... zu behalten', 'es ist so einfach wie ...', 'gestern Abend', 'sie waren *wo?*', 'morgen geht es mir (wieder) gut', 'morgen wird es (das Wetter) schön' und 'wir sind kurz nach neun dort'.

Forms of *be:* three, two, one

All my friends say it's
easy to remember the
forms of *be*:

three for the present,
two for the past,
one for the future.
It's as easy as one, two,
three.

For the **present** you have
am, are, is.

For the **past** you have
was and ***were***:

Yesterday evening *I was*
and *you were,*
she was and *we were,*
he was and *they were....*
They were *where*? – They
were there.

Will be is for the **future**,
or ***'ll be*** for short:
Tomorrow *I'll be,*
you'll be, she'll be,
he'll be, it'll be fine.
And *we'll be, you'll be,*
they'll be there just after
nine.

Sieh dir den Hinweis und die unvollständige Tabelle an. Lege in deinem Übungsheft eine Tabelle für die *past*- und *future*-Formen von *be* an.

forms of *be*			
the past		**the future**	
I was	ich war / (bin gewesen)	I'll be	ich werde sein / (ich bin)
you were	du warst / (bist gewesen)	you'll be	du wirst sein / (du bist)
she ...	...	she ...	sie wird sein / (sie ist)
...	...	...	...

In German we use two forms:
- for the past
  Gestern war ich ...
  Gestern bin ich gewesen ...
- for the future
  Morgen werde ich sein ...
  Morgen bin ich ...

Ergänze den unvollständigen Merksatz mithilfe des Merkverses von oben. Übertrage ihn dann in dein Übungsheft.

Man benötigt nur sechs Formen von *be*, um über Vergangenheit,
____________ und ____________ zu sprechen.
Die ________ für die Vergangenheit sind ________ und ________.
Für die Gegenwart benötigt man ________, ________ und ________.
Für die Zukunft genügt eine Form: ____________. Die Kurzform ist ____________.

4. an exercise

Lies den unvollständigen Text und ergänze dann die fehlenden Formen von *be*. (Die Lösung steht unter dem Text.)

Me and my new family

Hallo, I ______ Elmo. I ______ a member of Sue's family now. Sue ________ a retriever, and Billy ______ a boxer. They __________ my new parents.

Yesterday ________ the first day in my new family. Although the other dogs ________ nice to me, I ________ quite nervous. Now I ______ not so nervous any more.

Next weekend I __________ one year old. And on Saturday there ___________ a party for me. All my new friends ___________ there.

'm, 'm, is, is, are, was, were, was, 'm, 'll be, will be, will be

Sieh dir die Fragen an und finde heraus, was die Hundeeltern wissen möchten.

Finde die englischen Entsprechungen für 'die ganze Nacht', 'schlecht gelaunt', 'Warst du lange auf?', 'Bist du vor Mitternacht zu Hause?', 'auf die Welpen aufpassen', 'den ganzen Tag' und 'ich brauche eure Hilfe'.

Markiere, wie in den Beispielen, die Fragewörter (*where, ...*), die Formen von *be* (*was, ...*) und die Subjekte (*Elmo, ...*).

Hier hast du zwei Tabellen mit Fragen über die Vergangenheit und Zukunft. Übertrage sie in dein Übungsheft und ergänze sie mit den Beispielen aus dem Text.

Vervollständige diesen Merksatz, nachdem du den Hinweis darunter sorgfältig gelesen hast. Übertrage den Merksatz dann in dein Übungsheft.

5. talking about the past and the future: questions

As in all families: Parents ask questions, questions, questions.

Where was Elmo last night? His basket was empty. **Was he** with his friends all night?

Why were you in a bad mood this morning? Were you up late last night?

It's dangerous to go to the park alone. Why wasn't Katie with you? Wasn't she here when you left?

Where will you be tonight? **Will you be** home before midnight?

When will Katie be home tomorrow? Will she be here to look after the puppies?

Why will you be out all day? I need your help! – Will nobody be here tomorrow to help me?

Why won't the puppies be back for lunch? Won't they be hungry?

questions to talk about the past:	questions to talk about the future:
Where was Elmo last night?	Where will you be tonight?
Was he ...	Will you be ...
Why ...	When ...
...	...

Der Satzbauplan für ______________ mit *be* über die Vergangenheit ist:

(Fragewort) + __________/__________ + Subjekt + ...?

Der __________________ für Fragen über die ____________ ist:

(______________) + ______ + Subjekt + *be* + ...?

Verneinte Fragen bildest du mit ________ und *weren't* für die Vergangenheit und _____________ für die Zukunft.

- The **word order** for questions about the past: (question word) + *was/were* + subject + ...?
- The **word order** for questions about the future: (question word) + *will* + subject + *be* + ...?
- You can also make negative questions with *wasn't/weren't* for the past and *won't be* for the future.

Lies diesen Text und finde heraus, wie sich Sue fühlte.

Finde die englischen Entsprechungen für 'Putztag', 'ich weiß nicht, warum ...', 'es war mir nicht möglich zu ...', '(sie) werden sich nicht freuen'.

Markiere, wie in den Beispielen, die Vergangenheits- und die Zukunftsformen für *be*.

6. talking about the past and the future: negative statements

Monday, 29 February

Today was a terrible day. It was my cleaning day. The older children **weren't** here to help me. I don't know why they weren't at home. And Billy? Well, he wasn't interested! He was in front of the TV again. – It wasn't possible for me to clean the whole house. I'll do the rest tomorrow. I hope the big children **won't be** out again. If nobody helps me, there won't be any food tomorrow. Billy and the children won't be happy. But it will not be possible to clean the house and do the shopping. ...

Sue's diary

HINT

- The two negative forms of *be* for the past are *wasn't* and *weren't*.
- The negative form for the future is *won't be*. The long form is *will not be*.

Die zwei ____________ Formen von *be* für die Vergangenheit sind ____________ und *weren't*. Die verneinte ____________ von *be* für die Zukunft ist *won't be*. Die Langform ist ____________.

Sieh dir den unvollständigen Merksatz und den Hinweis an. Vervollständige dann den Merksatz und übertrage ihn in dein Übungsheft.

7. from the past to the present: another form of *be* (present perfect)

Lies, was Elmo über sein neues Leben sagt und finde heraus, wie er sich jetzt fühlt.

Finde die englischen Entsprechungen für 'bis letzte Woche', 'seit einer Woche', 'seit letzter Woche', 'die ganze Woche' und 'ein so guter Vater'.

Suche weitere *present perfect* Formen (bejahte und verneinte sowie Fragen) im Text und markiere sie.

Until last week …
… I had no home. I was often hungry. I was often dirty.
But look at me now. **I haven't been** hungry for a week.
I haven't been dirty for a week. Since last week my life has been totally different. Life hasn't been this good for a long time.
– Why?
Well, … **I have been** a member of a new family since last week. Sue has been so nice to me all week. And Billy has been such a good father to me. – I ask myself every minute: **Have I been** in a dream for a week or has this been real?

Sieh dir die Tabelle und die zwei Hinweise darunter an. Übertrage dann die Tabelle in dein Übungsheft und ergänze sie mit den Formen aus dem Text.

positive statements	negative statements	questions
have been	…	…?
… been	hasn't …	… has this been …?

- You make the present perfect of *be* with *have/has + been*.
- You make the negative form with *haven't/hasn't + been*.
- You use the present perfect to speak about the time from the past to the present. See *45 tenses (2)*.

HINT

Remember:
- infinitive: *be*
- past participle: *been*

8. a problem for you?

Vergleiche die englischen Sätze in der Tabelle mit ihren deutschen Entsprechungen. Weshalb, denkst du, können die Verbformen und Satzbaupläne Lernenden Probleme bereiten?

Übertrage die Tabelle in dein Übungsheft und markiere die Verbformen wie in den Beispielen.

the past	from the past to the present	the present
I **was** often unhappy.	I **have been** happy **for a week now**.	I**'m** happy **now**.
Ich **war** oft unglücklich. Ich **bin** oft unglücklich **gewesen**.	Ich **bin jetzt seit einer Woche** glücklich.	Ich **bin jetzt** glücklich.

Ordne die weiteren sechs Sätze jeweils einer der Spalten zu.

Six more sentences:

Billy wasn't unfriendly when I arrived.

Were you in a dream last week?

He hasn't been unfriendly all week.

Are you in a dream?

Billy isn't unfriendly.

Have you been in a dream since last week?

12 can

das Verb *can* (können)

Sieh dir diesen Text an und finde heraus, was Haie tun oder nicht tun können.

Finde die englischen Entsprechungen für 'Blut auf einen Kilometer riechen', 'Meeresschildkröte', 'in einer Stellung verharren', 'auf dem Meeresboden', 'eine Reihe anderer Haie' und 'Schwimmblase'.

Markiere, wie in den drei Beispielsätzen, jeweils das Subjekt, *can/can't* und das Vollverb. Übertrage dann die Sätze in drei Tabellen in dein Übungsheft.

Can is a 'special' verb: It is a modal. – You can find out more about modal verbs at *18 modals*.

1. word order in statements and questions

Sharks – as old as the dinosaurs

Sharks can smell blood from one kilometre.
A tiger shark can bite through a large turtle.
Sharks can't stay in one position.
A shark can't lie on the sea bed and rest.

Frequently Asked Questions ...	... and Answers:
Can a shark feel the fear of other fish?	Yes, it can.
Can sharks attack people?	They can. But most sharks are not dangerous.
Can I see a tiger shark here in the aquarium?	No, you can't. But we can show you a number of other sharks.
What can a shark eat?	It can eat other fish.
Why can't sharks stay in one position?	They don't have a swim bladder.

positive statements
Sharks can smell ...
A tiger shark ...
...

negative statements
Sharks can't stay...
...

questions
Can a shark feel ...?
– Yes, it can.
...

Sieh dir den Hinweis rechts sowie den unvollständigen Merksatz an. Ergänze dann den Merksatz und übertrage ihn in dein Übungsheft.

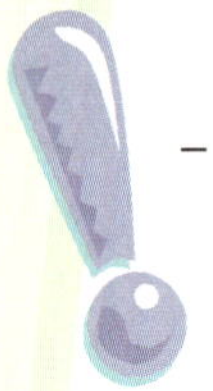

– In bejahten Aussagesätzen verwendet man für alle ______________ *can*.
– In ________________ Aussagesätzen verwendet man für _________ Personen ________; manchmal siehst du die Form *cannot* ['kænɒt].
– Für bejahte und ________________ Aussagesätze ist der Satzbauplan ______________ + *can/can't* + ____________________.
– Der _______________________ für Fragen ist (Fragewort +) _________/__________ + Subjekt + Vollverb.

Forms of *can*:
– In positive statements you use *can* for <u>all</u> persons.
– In negative statements you use *can't* for <u>all</u> persons.

Word order
– In positive and negative statements: subject + *can/can't* + main verb.
– In questions: (question word +) *can/can't* + subject + main verb.

Normally you pronounce *can* as [kən]. But in short answers and questions you use the strong form [kæn].

2. word order: a problem for you?

Vergleiche die englischen und deutschen Satzbaupläne. Übertrage die Sätze in dein Übungsheft und markiere sie wie in den Beispielen. Übertrage auch die weiteren vier Sätze und ergänze die deutschen Entsprechungen.

Sharks	can	swim.	
Haie	können	schwimmen.	
Sharks	can	swim	well.
Haie	können	gut	schwimmen.

<u>More sentences</u>: Sharks can smell blood from 1 kilometre. Sharks can't stay in one position. Can sharks attack people? Why can't sharks stay in one position?

3. the different meanings of *can*

Plymouth Aquarium –
a note for Year 7 pupils

1. The coach leaves at 9 am. We can't wait, so don't be late.
2. Bring a pullover. It can be quite cold in the aquarium.
3. You can work in groups and learn about different sharks.
4. I hope everyone can remember what they must find out about the fish.
5. Ask a teacher for help if you can't answer a question.
6. You can't take photos of all the fish. It's not good for some of them.
7. Finally, can you please behave yourselves on the trip.

Du kannst *can* verwenden, um auszudrücken, dass…

a. jemand *fähig* ist, etwas zu tun
b. jemand *nicht fähig* ist, etwas zu tun
c. etwas *möglich* ist
d. etwas *nicht möglich* ist
e. etwas *erlaubt* ist
f. etwas *nicht erlaubt* ist
g. du um etwas *bitten* willst.

Lies den Merkzettel für den Ausflug nach Plymouth und finde die englischen Entsprechungen für 'kommt also nicht zu spät', 'ziemlich kalt', 'ich hoffe, dass sich jeder merken kann, …', 'Photos machen' und 'könnt ihr euch bitte benehmen'.

Sieh dir die Liste mit den verschiedenen Bedeutungen von *can* und den Text an. Verbinde dann die zusammengehörigen Sätze. (Die Lösung steht unten.)

4. talking about the past, the present and the future

What it was like at the aquarium last Saturday.
You **could get** a ticket at 9 o'clock. You could walk around and you could see everything.
Later, you couldn't get a ticket and you couldn't get in. Too many buses had arrived.

What it is like today at Plymouth Aquarium.
You **can get** a ticket quite easily. You can walk around and you can see everything.
You can't get a ticket so easily during the school holidays and you can't see everything.

What it will be like next month.
If you come early, you **will be able to get** a ticket to see sea horses from all over the world.
You will be able to learn why they are in danger.
You won't be able to get a ticket if you come late.

past – could …
…

present – can get
can't …

future – will be able to …
…

In diesen Texten erhalten Besucher weitere Auskunft über das *Plymouth Aquarium*. Markiere die Formen von *can* + *Vollverb* für Vergangenheit, Gegenwart und Zukunft.

Übertrage die Formen in drei Tabellen, wie in dem Beispiel, in dein Übungsheft .

5. *could*: talking about the past and about the future

I enjoyed it so much, I could go again …
We went to Plymouth Aquarium last week.
We could walk around and watch the sharks.
We could see a turtle in the shark tank,too.
I couldn't believe my eyes when two divers jumped into the shark tank. They could swim among the sharks and feed them.
I could spend another day there next week.
I could ask my parents to take us.
We could arrive before the crowds. And then I could see all the fish that I couldn't see last week.

talking about the past
We could walk …
…

talking about the future
I could spend …
…

Sieh dir zunächst den Text an. Entscheide für jeden Satz mit *could*, ob über Vergangenheit oder Zukunft gesprochen wird. Lege in deinem Übungsheft zwei Tabellen an, in die du die Sätze einträgst.

The word *could* has two meanings in German:
It is *konnte/n* (to talk about the past) and *könnte/n* (to talk about the future).

Mit *could* kann man über Vergangenheit und ______________ sprechen.
Spricht man über die ______________________, so entspricht *could* dem Deutschen *konnte*. Spricht man über die __________________, dann entspricht *could* dem Deutschen ______________.

Lies den Hinweis und ergänze dann den Merksatz. Übertrage ihn in dein Übungsheft.

1d, 2c, 3e, 4a, 5b, 6f, 7g

13 conjunctions

Conjunctions are words that can link words, parts of sentences, clauses or sentences.

Konjunktionen

Sieh dir den unvollständigen Text über *Die lustigen Mädchen* an und finde heraus, weshalb die jungen Leute von einem Geiger enttäuscht wurden.

Versuche diese Konjunktionen sinnvoll in den Text einzusetzen:

after – *nachdem*
and – *und*
as soon as – *sobald*
because – *weil*
until – *bis*
when – *als*
(Die Lösung steht unten auf der Seite.)

Finde die englischen Entsprechungen für 'es gibt eine Sage über…', 'lange feiern', 'bis der Tag sich neigte' und 'als es Mitternacht war'.

1. a legend without conjunctions

In Britain there are many stone circles. One stone circle in Cornwall is called the Merry Maidens. And there is a legend about this stone circle …

The Merry Maidens

Many years ago there was a wedding in a village. All the young people went to a field to celebrate. ____________ it was Saturday, they decided to celebrate late. ____________ they had eaten, they asked a fiddler to play his music. Everybody began to dance ____________ the music started. They danced ________ danced ____________ the day turned to night. ____________ midnight came, the fiddler stopped. 'I cannot play on Sunday,' he said and left.

Schreibe diese Sätze – mit der deutschen Entsprechung für die Nebensätze – in dein Übungsheft.
Vergleiche die englischen und deutschen Satzbaupläne und markiere alle Unterschiede.

Wo, denkst du, könnten Lernende Probleme haben?

2. word order: a problem for you?

Suddenly, a tall dark figure appeared **who** played the fiddle.
…, die die Geige …
If this man played for them, the villagers could dance all night.
Wenn …
The people realized **that** this was no ordinary fiddler.
…, dass …
Although he looked like a fiddler, everybody felt that he was different.
Obwohl …
But nobody asked **if** the fiddler was the Devil.
Aber … , ob …

Sieh dir den Kasten mit Konjunktionen und den Lückentext an. Vervollständige ihn mit den Konjunktionen. (Die Lösung steht unter dem Text.)

Übertrage alle Konjunktionen auf dieser Seite in alphabetischer Reihenfolge in dein Übungsheft.

Conjunctions	
English	German
after	nachdem
although	…

3. an exercise: the end of the legend

until • but • since *(weil)* • when • before *(bevor)* • where *(wo)* • and • and

HINT

- If you start with a conjunction, put a comma after the clause.
- There is normally no comma if the conjunction is in the middle of a sentence.
- There is usually a comma before *but* and *or*: *They asked him, but he said …*
- There is no comma before *that*: *He said that …*

They asked who he was ________ where he came from, ________ he gave no answer. Suddenly they knew: It was the Devil. __________ the morning came, there was a stone circle in the field ________ the people had been. The Devil laughed. "I have this to say ____________ I go. ____________ you didn't listen to the fiddler, I have turned you to stone. One day I will return ________ I will play again for you. __________ that day comes, you must all wait – frozen in stone."

Part 1: because, after, as soon as, and, until, when
Part 3: and, but, when, where, before, since, and, until

14 the date: days, months, years

das Datum: Tage, Monate, Jahre

1. jumbled days and months

Sieh dir diese 'Wörter' an.

Bringe die Buchstaben in die richtige Reihenfolge und übertrage die Wörter in zwei Tabellen *(months/days of the week)* in dein Übungsheft. (Die Lösung steht unten auf der Seite.)

weekdays

dTyrhusa
nyMdoa
aWneddsey
yFaird
seyuTda

the weekend

aunydS – Sdtauary

winter

raunJay
mebceDer
urarbeFy

spring

raMch
liprA
yaM

summer

luyJ
neJu
stugAu

autumn

bermetpeS
merbvoNe
robetOc

2. dates: what you may hear and what you may see written down

Lies diese sechs Texte und finde die englischen Entsprechungen für '(er) ist 1915 geboren', '(sie) ist am ... in ... bei einem Autounfall gestorben', '(See)reise', 'die versunkene Stadt Atlantis' und 'du findest vielleicht'.

Finde die Datumsangabe zu jedem Text, ergänze diese und verbinde Text und Datum.

The computer specialist JCR Licklider, one of the 'fathers' of the internet, was born in nineteen fifteen and died in nineteen ninety.

Princess Diana died in a car crash in Paris on Sunday, the thirty-first of August, nineteen ninety-seven.

The Titanic sank on its first voyage on the fourteenth of April, nineteen twelve.

Sunday, 08/___/______

01/___/______

Sunday, 31 August, ______

____/04/____

______ – 1990

20/07/______

Some people think the lost city of Atlantis will be found on January the first, two thousand and twenty.

Neil Armstrong first stood on the moon on July the twentieth, nineteen sixty-nine.

In some American books you may find the date of Diana's crash with the month first, then the day and finally the year.

- *in* + year or month *(in 1999, in May)*
- *on* + day *(on 20 July or: on July 20, on Saturday, on 14 May, 1912)*
- You write: you say:

You write	you say
1901	*nineteen O one*
1999	*nineteen ninety-nine*
2000	*two thousand*
2002	*two thousand and two*

1551	fifteen ...
1616	sixteen ...
1969	...
20/07/1969	July the ...
...	
01/01/2020	...
...	...

Übertrage den Hinweis in dein Übungsheft und lege dir eine Tabelle an, in die du einträgst, wie du Jahreszahl und Datum sagen kannst.

3. public holidays

Finde heraus, wie diese Feiertage auf Deutsch heißen, bzw. wann was gefeiert wird. Schreibe sie mit Datum in der richtigen Reihenfolge in dein Übungsheft.

Easter
Christmas Eve/~ Day
Boxing Day
Mawlid al-Nabi (Islamic)
Eid al-Fidr (Islamic)

Rosh Hashana (Jewish)
Yom Kippur (Jewish)
Diwali (Hindu)
Holi (Hindu)
German Unification

Thanksgiving (USA)
Independence Day (USA)
New Year's Day
Valentine's Day
Halloween

Monday, Tuesday, Wednesday, Thursday, Friday, Saturday, Sunday; January, February, March, April, May, June, July, August, September, October, November, Dececember

das Verb *do* (tun/machen)

Sieh dir das Bild und den Text an und finde heraus, was das Mädchen zu erzählen hat. Finde dann die englischen Entsprechungen für 'ich mache gerade meine Hausaufgaben', 'ich mache das morgen früh', 'ich mache das, sobald ...', 'sie hat ein paar Kunststückchen gemacht' und 'er hat seine Aufgaben erledigt'.

Im Text sind sieben Subjekte und Formen von *do* markiert. Finde neun weitere Subjekte mit Formen von *do* und markiere sie.

15 do

Do is a very common verb in English. Here you can learn how to use it as a *main verb*.

1. *do* as a main verb: positive statements

"We can't go out. **I'm doing** my homework now. Tom is doing some jobs for dad. They're doing something in the garden."

"We've ruined our bikes. **We did** it yesterday. Sue did some tricks with her bike, I did some tricks, then we crashed into each other."

So much to tell!

"I'm busy now. I'll bring your games back, I promise. **I'll do** it tomorrow morning. **I'm going to do** it as soon as I get up."

"**Luke and I usually do** our homework together on Saturday. He often does it at my house. I sometimes do it at his house."

"**I might do** a project for school today. We can do something tomorrow. Do your homework now if you're bored."

"My brother and I've been busy since breakfast. **I've done** all my jobs. My brother has done his jobs. We can go out now."

In dieser Tabelle findest du Formen des *simple past, present perfect, present progressive, simple present* sowie Futur- und Modalformen. Die markierten Formen im Text und der Hinweis helfen dir, die Tabelle zu ergänzen.

Übertrage die Tabelle und den Hinweis in dein Übungsheft.

forms of *do*

the past	from the past to the present	the present	the future
did	*have* ________	*am doing*	*will* ________ **or**
	________ *done*	*are doing*	________ *going to do*
		________ *doing*	*are going to do*
			is ____________ *do*

with modals: ________ *do*, ________ *do*

permanent situations: *do*/____________

To give an order, you can say:
Do your homework.
Don't be late.

for **all** persons
- *did*
- *will do*
- *can do, might do*

for **he, she, it**
- *has done*
- *does*

for **be**
- I *am*
- we, you, they *are*
- he, she it *is*

2. some expressions with *do*

Sieh dir die Lückensätze, ihre deutsche Entsprechung und die sechs Formen von *do* an.
Verbinde die zusammengehörigen Sätze. Übertrage die Satzpaare in dein Übungsheft und ergänze dabei jeweils die richtige Form von *do*.
(Die Lösungen stehen unter den Sätzen.)

do • did • is doing • does • 'll do • has done

1. Tom ... a lot of work at the moment.
2. We ... our best, but it wasn't enough.
3. Charlie often ... the shopping for us.
4. ... some exercise. It's good for you.
5. We ... the housework tomorrow.
6. Carol ... nothing since she got up.

- Wir erledigen die Hausarbeit morgen.
- Carol hat, seit sie aufgestanden ist, nichts getan.
- Wir haben unser Bestes getan, aber es war nicht genug.
- Beweg dich ein bisschen. Das wird dir gut tun.
- Tom arbeitet im Augenblick eine Menge.
- Charlie geht oft für uns einkaufen.

1. is doing; 2. did; 3. does; 4. Do; 5. will do; 6. has done

3. *do* as a main verb: negative statements

A difficult decision

I'm doing well in History this year.
I think I'll do that next year.
I'm not doing well in Geography.
I won't do that.
I did well in PE last year,
so I might do that.
I didn't do well in Music,
so I might not do that.
I usually do well in practical subjects.
And I don't do so well in languages.
So I'm not going to do another foreign language next year. I'm going to do Art instead.
I haven't done Media Studies before. I might do that.
But I can't do Art if I do Media Studies.
Oh no, …

A subject guide for years 10 & 11

Pupils must take all the core subjects. They must choose four options.

Core subjects: English, Maths, Science, one Foreign Language, Religious Education, Physical Education (PE)

Options: History, Geography, Art, Media Studies, PE, Technology, French, German, Music, IT, Russian, Italian, Japanese, Astronomy

Der Text und der Handzettel helfen dir herauszufinden, welche schwierige Entscheidung das Mädchen zu treffen hat.

Finde die englischen Entsprechungen für 'Kernfächer', 'Wahlpflichtfächer', 'ich bin (dieses Jahr) in Erdkunde nicht gut' und 'ich bin (gewöhnlich) in Sprachen nicht so gut'.

Im Text sind je zwei Subjekte und Formen von *do* markiert. Finde weitere zwölf bejahte bzw. verneinte Formen von *do* und markiere sie.

negative forms of *do*

the past	from the past to the present	the present	the future
_________ *do*	________ *done*	*'m* ______ *doing*	__________ *do* or
	hasn't ________	*aren't* _________	*'m* ______________ *to do*
		isn't _________	*aren't going to do*
			isn't ______________ *do*

with modals: *might not do*, _________ *do*

permanent situations: ___________ *do/doesn't* ___________

Sieh dir die Tabelle, den Hinweis und die Formen von *do* im Text an. Vervollständige die Tabelle mit den verneinten Formen von *do* und übertrage sie zusammen mit dem Hinweis in dein Übungsheft.

When the verb has **more than one part** *(have done, can do)*,
add **…*n't*** or ***not*** **behind the first part** *(haven't done, can't do, might not do)*.

4. *do* as a main verb: questions

What are you doing, Emma? Are you doing French now or German?

You haven't chosen your options yet. Why do you always do things at the last minute? Does your sister do everything so late?

What is Sue doing? Is she doing Art or Media Studies?

Simon, did you do Geography last year? Was it easy? Why did you do it? Did Sam do the same subjects as you?

Have you ever done Japanese before? Are you sure you'll like it?

Has Zoe done all the things she must do?

In diesen Sprechblasen sind drei Formen markiert. Sie zeigen, wie man Fragen mit *do* als Vollverb bildet. Finde weitere acht Beispiele und markiere sie.

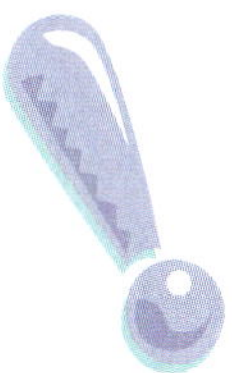

Besteht die Verbform von *do* aus zwei oder mehr Teilen *(have done/are* _________*/is going to* ________*)*, kommt der erste Teil vor das Subjekt: ________ *you done …?/are they* _________ *…?/is she* _________ *to do …?*

Wenn die Verbform nur aus ____________ Teil besteht *(do, does, did)*, sagt man: ________ *you do …?/does she* _______ *…?/did they* _______ *…?*

Lies den unvollständigen Merksatz und sieh dir die Beispiele an. Vervollständige dann den Merksatz und übertrage ihn in dein Übungsheft.

das Verb *have* (haben)

Lies den Text und die Sprechblase und finde heraus, welches Problem viele Menschen heute haben und wie es vielleicht gelöst wird.

Suche nun die englischen Entsprechungen für 'Faxgeräte', 'Handys', 'zu viele, als dass man sie sich merken könnte', 'überall auf der Welt' und 'Ich habe dieses Telefon erst seit einer Woche'.

Im Text und der Sprechblase sind acht Subjekte mit Formen von *have* markiert. Finde sechs weitere Subjekte mit Formen von *have* und markiere sie.

Sieh dir die markierten Formen von *have*, den Hinweis und die Tabelle an. In der Tabelle findest du Formen des *simple past, present perfect und simple present* sowie Futur- und Modalformen.

Vervollständige dann die Tabelle und übertrage sie und den Hinweis in dein Übungsheft.

16 have

Have, together with *be* and *do*, is one of the most common verbs in English.

1. *have* as a main verb: positive statements

Modern technology

Before fax machines, mobile phones and the internet, **people had** one number: their telephone number. When fax machines and mobile phones arrived, many people suddenly had two, or even three numbers.

Today **many people have** e-mail and an internet address. **Their e-mail has** an ISP address, their website has a URL. So they have at least five different numbers and addresses. – Too many to remember.

Experts say **we might have** a new system in the 21st century. We can have just one number again, for all our machines, everywhere in the world. And nobody should have a problem with one number!

Soon **some companies are going to have** the new system. These telecommunication companies hope **they will have** lots of new customers. – And their customers hope they will have cheaper phone bills!

I've only had this phone for a week and it's broken. **My sister has had** her phone for over a year and nothing is wrong with it.

forms of *have*			
the past	from the past to the present	the present	the future
________	*have* ________	________	*will* ________ or
	________ *had*	*has*	*'m going to have*
			________ *going to have*
			is ____________ *have*
		with modals: ______, ______, *might have*	

for **all** persons
- *had*
- *will have*
- *can, should, might have*

for **he, she, it**
- *has had*
- *has*

for **be**
- I *am*
- we, you, they *are*
- he, she it *is*

For more about the short forms of *have*, see *22 long forms/ short forms*.

2. some expressions with *have*

Lies die Lückensätze und die deutschen Entsprechungen. Verbinde dann die zusammengehörigen Sätze. Übertrage die Satzpaare in dein Übungsheft und ergänze die Formen von *have*. (Die Lösung steht unter den Sätzen.)

1. Tom … no idea about technology.
2. Yesterday he … problems with his computer.
3. We … a 24-hour-hotline since last year.
4. You … time to read your e-mails tomorrow.
5. I … a fax machine, but I don't want one.

- Ich sollte ein Faxgerät haben, aber ich möchte keines.
- Wir haben seit letztem Jahr eine 24-Stunden-Hotline.
- Du hast morgen Zeit, deine E-Mails zu lesen.
- Tom hat von Technik keine Ahnung.
- Er hatte gestern Probleme mit seinem Computer.

1. has; 2. had; 3. have had; 4. 'll have ; 5. should have

3. *have* as a main verb: negative statements

Sieh dir die Sprechblasen an und finde die englischen Entsprechungen für 'vor einigen Jahren', 'Internetzugang', 'seit zwei Jahren', 'bisher' und 'Batterien, die nach zwei Stunden leer sind'.

In den Sprechblasen sind vier Subjekte mit Formen von *have* markiert. Finde weitere zwölf bejahte und verneinte Formen von *have* und markiere sie.

We had an old mobile phone several years ago. **It didn't have** a mailbox or internet access. We didn't have it very long.

We've had the same mobile phone for two years. **I haven't had** any problems so far. My boyfriend hasn't had any difficulties either.

My parents don't have a mobile phone. They have a fax machine with a phone. My grandmother doesn't have a fax. She has a computer.

Mobile phones

A cheap phone can't have the same standby time as an expensive phone. But it shouldn't have batteries that are flat after two hours.

I'll have a new mobile soon. It'll have software for the internet. I hope I won't have any problems with it. I'm not going to have a very expensive phone.

negative forms of *have*

the past	from the past to the present	the present	the future
didn't ________	*haven't* ________	*don't* ________	*won't* ________ **or**
	________ *had*	________ *have*	*'m not going to have*
			________ *going to have*
			isn't ________ *have*
with modals: ________, ________ *have*			

Ergänze diese unvollständige Tabelle mit verneinten Formen von *have*. Die markierten Formen in den fünf Sprechblasen oben helfen dir dabei. Übertrage die Tabelle in dein Übungsheft.

4. *have* as a main verb: questions

Lies zunächst, was die verschiedenen Leute wissen möchten. Die markierten Formen zeigen dir, wie man Fragen mit dem Vollverb *have* bildet. Finde weitere sieben Beispiele für Fragen mit *have* in diesen Sätzen und markiere sie.

When did you have your first computer? Did it really have no hard drive?

How long has Sue had her own website?

Do you have e-mail?

Why does Tom have two email addresses?

Could I have a virus on my hard drive?

Is Tom going to have a DVD player with his new computer?

What anti-virus program should I have for my computer?

When will you have a DVD player?

Besteht die Verbform von *have* aus zwei oder mehr Teilen (*have*[1] *had*[2]/*is going to* ________/*can* ________), kommt der erste Teil vor das Subjekt: *have* ________ *had …?/is he* ________ *to have …?/can I* ________ *…?*
Besteht die ________ aus nur ________ Teil (*have*[1], *has, had*), sagt man: *do you have …?/*________ *she have …?/did they* ________ *…?*

Sieh dir den unvollständigen Merksatz zur Bildung von Fragen mit *have* als Vollverb und die Beispiele in den Sprechblasen an. Vervollständige ihn und übertrage ihn dann in dein Übungsheft.

Sieh dir die deutschen Sätze an und finde jeweils den entsprechenden englischen Lückensatz. Schreibe die jeweilige Zahl vor den Satz.
Finde dann in dem gelben Kasten die passende Form von *have* für jeden Satz und trage sie ein. (Die Lösung steht unten auf der Seite.)

Übertrage die englischen Sätze mit ihren deutschen Entsprechungen in dein Übungsheft.

don't ... have • had • 'll have • haven't had • 'm having • have • didn't have • ~~have~~

5. *have* + noun = activity

8 ___*Have*___ a cup of tea. It'll do you good.

_ I only ________ a sandwich yesterday.

_ Can I phone you back? I ______________ dinner at the moment.

_ We always __________ lunch at one.

_ I _________________ my breakfast yet.

_ We _____________ a snack later.

_ I ________ usually _________ coffee in the morning.

_ I _________________ any breakfast yesterday. At 10 o'clock I was starving.

1. Ich trinke normalerweise morgens keinen Kaffee.
2. Wir essen immer um eins zu Mittag.
3. Ich habe gestern nur ein Sandwich gegessen.
4. Ich habe gestern nicht gefrühstückt. Um 10 Uhr bin ich halb verhungert.
5. Ich habe noch nicht gefrühstückt.
6. Wir essen später eine Kleinigkeit.
7. Kann ich dich zurückrufen? Ich esse gerade zu Abend.
8. Trink eine Tasse Tee. Das tut dir gut.

6. a problem for you?

Sieh dir die Bilder und die drei Sprechblasen an.
In den Sprechblasen sind sechs Ausdrücke mit *have* + *noun* markiert.
Übertrage die Sätze ins Deutsche und benutze dabei die Verben 'baden', 'duschen' und 'haben'. – Weshalb, denkst du, haben Lernende mit diesen Formen häufig Probleme?

7. some more useful expressions with *have* + noun

Übertrage diese Ausdrücke mit *have* + *noun* in dein Übungsheft.
Finde in den Sprechblasen oben weitere Ausdrücke mit *have* + *noun* und füge sie hinzu.

have a wash	*sich waschen*
a shower	*(sich) duschen*
a bath	*(sich) baden*
a shave	*sich rasieren*
a haircut	*sich die Haare schneiden lassen*

have a walk	*spazieren gehen*
have a look at	*sich etwas ansehen*
have a baby	*ein Baby bekommen*
Have a try.	*Versuch's mal.*
Have a go.	*Mach's/Tu's mal.*

have a conversation about — *sich unterhalten über*
have a discussion about — *diskutieren über*

have a letter from	*einen Brief ...*
an e-mail from	*eine E-Mail ...*
a phone call from	*einen Anruf ... bekommen von*

have, had, 'm having, have, haven't had, 'll have, don't ... have, didn't have

17 have got/has got

1. positive statements, negative statements, questions

Have got and *has got* can have the same meaning as *have* and *has*, but you only use them to talk about the present.

Excuses, excuses …

die Formen *have got* und *has got*

Sieh dir die sechs Sprechblasen an und finde die englischen Entsprechungen für 'ich nehme an', 'Ausreden', 'furchtbares Kopfweh', 'er hat eine Erkältung' 'Turnschuhe', 'noch eine faule Ausrede' und 'Können wir jetzt Sport machen?'

In den Sprechblasen sind drei Formen von *have got* und *has got* markiert. Finde weitere fünf bejahte und zwei verneinte Formen sowie drei Fragen mit *have got* und *has got* und markiere sie.

short form — long form

positive statements		negative statements		questions		
I / you / we / they	've got / have ______	I / you / we / they	______ got	______	I / you / we / they	got …?
she / he / it	's got / ______ got	she / he / it	______	______	she / he / it	______ …?
				______		has got …?

Sieh dir diese unvollständige Tabelle an. Vervollständige sie und übertrage sie in dein Übungsheft.

Die Formen *have got* und ________ *got* kann man nur verwenden, um über die ________________ zu sprechen.

Wenn man über die Vergangenheit oder die ________________ sprechen möchte, benötigt man die Formen des Vollverbs *have*.

HINT

If you want to speak about the past or the future, you need the forms of the full verb *have*. See pages 30 and 31 for these forms.

Sieh dir den unvollständigen Merksatz, den Hinweis daneben und den Hinweis oben an. Vervollständige dann den Merksatz und übertrage ihn in dein Übungsheft.

2. *have got* or *has got*: positive or negative form?

1. Don't hurry. We ____________ plenty of time.
2. Sandra ________________ enough money. She needs another 50p.
3. If you ______________ toothache, go to the dentist.
4. Tim __________ a new haircut. It's cool.
5. I _________________ any trainers. I can't play.
6. Carl ______________________ any ideas.

Vervollständige nun diese Sätze mit einer bejahten oder verneinten Form von *have got* oder *has got*, so dass sich sinnvolle Aussagen ergeben. (Die Lösung steht unter den Sätzen.)

1. have got; 2. hasn't got; 3. have got; 4. has got; 5. haven't got; 6. hasn't got

18 have to

das Verb *have to* (müssen)

Have to has the same meaning as *must*. But it has forms to talk about the past and the future.

1. *have to*: positive statements

Sieh dir den Text und die Sprechblase an und finde heraus, weshalb die Bahnfahrt von London auf den Kontinent nicht mehr so mühsam ist.

Suche nun die englischen Entsprechungen für 'die Bahnfahrt dauerte endlos lang', 'Zoll und Passkontrolle', 'jeder musste noch einmal das gleiche tun', 'niemand muss durch den Zoll gehen', 'sie müssen möglicherweise eine ganz neue Trasse bauen' und 'ich habe entscheiden müssen, wie ...'.

Im Text und der Sprechblase sind fünf Subjekte und Formen von *have to* + *infinitive* markiert. Finde sechs weitere Subjekte mit Formen von *have to* + *infinitive* und markiere sie.

Crossing the Channel by train

In the past the train journey from Britain to the Continent was endless: **You had to take** a train to Dover and leave it there. Then passengers had to go through British customs and passport control and get onto a ferry.

In the last three months **my firm has had to send** me to France once a week. I've had to decide how to travel, by train or by plane.

At the other side of the Channel everybody had to do the same again: Go through customs, show their passports, get on a train ...

Today it is different because of the Channel Tunnel and Eurostar, a high-speed train: **You only have to check in** at London Waterloo Station, get on the train and wait until Eurostar arrives in Brussels or Paris. Nobody has to go through customs when it gets to the Channel or when it has travelled through the Channel Tunnel. There is only one problem: Eurostar has to travel quite slowly from London to Dover. There is no high-speed railway line.

Britain will have to build a fast line to make the journey shorter. **They might have to build** a totally new line for Eurostar. And they will have to do it soon. Or passengers will go by plane.

In dieser Tabelle findest du einige unvollständige Formen von *have to*. Ergänze sie mithilfe der markierten Formen im Text und der Information aus dem Hinweis. Übertrage die Tabelle und den Hinweis in dein Übungsheft.

forms of *have to*

the past	from the past to the present	the present	the future
________ *to*	*have* ________ *to*	____________	________ *have* _____
	_______ *had* ____	*has to*	
		with modals: ____________	*have* ______

HINT

for **all** persons
- *had to*
- *will have to*
- *might have to*

for **he, she, it**
- *has had to*
- *has to*

2. an exercise: some sentences with *have to* ...

Sieh dir diese Sätze und rechts die Formen von *have to* an. Übertrage die Sätze in dein Übungsheft und vervollständige sie mit je einer der Formen. (Die Lösung steht unter der Übung.)

1. You ... Waterloo Station if you want to travel by Eurostar from London.
2. Your name always ... on your ticket.
3. In the beginning Eurostar ... less than 80 km per hour from London to Dover.
4. Tim ... Paris ten times since May.
5. He ... Paris yesterday for an important meeting.
6. He ... London tomorrow to tell his boss about it.
7. If you smoke, you ... in carriage number 5.
8. We ... trains in Amsterdam, but it's not certain.

have to sit
'll have to return to
have to go to
might have to change
has to be
has had to go to
had to travel at
had to go to

1. have to go to; 2. has to be; 3. had to travel at; 4. has had to go to; 5. had to go to; 6. 'll have to return to; 7. have to sit; 8. might have to change

3. *have to*: negative sentences

Travelling from one country to another

In the past **people had to show** their passports at every European border.
Liz travelled from Amsterdam to Frankfurt last week.
She didn't have to show her passport at all.

At airports **passengers have had to go** through security checks since the 1960s. Most passengers haven't had to open their luggage. For a long time scanners have been used to see what is inside. Liz has travelled by plane many times. So far she hasn't had to open her luggage.

For some countries you don't have to have a passport. You only have to have an identity card. A German person, for example, doesn't have to use a passport within the European Union.

In the future you won't have to show a passport anywhere. You will have to look into a machine. This machine will identify you. In a hundred years you might not have to have a passport. You might have to have a bar code to be identified.

Das Bild und der Text helfen dir herauszufinden, wie sich Reisen verändert hat und vielleicht noch verändern wird.

Finde die englischen Entsprechungen für 'Liz reiste von ... nach...', 'sie musste ihren Pass nicht zeigen', 'seit den 60er-Jahren', 'seit langem', 'man benötigt nur einen Personalausweis' und 'in 100 Jahren braucht man vielleicht keinen Pass'.

Im Text sind drei Subjekte mit Formen von *have to + infinitive* markiert. Finde neun weitere bejahte bzw. verneinte Formen von *have to + infinitive* und markiere sie.

negative forms of *have to*

the past	from the past to the present	the present	the future
didn't ______ *to*	*haven't* ______ *to*	*don't* ______	*won't* ______
	______ *had* ______	______ *have to*	
		with modals: ______ *have to*	

Sieh dir diese unvollständige Tabelle mit verneinten Formen von *have to* und die markierten Stellen im Text an. Ergänze die fehlenden Formen und übertrage die Tabelle dann in dein Übungsheft.

4. *have to*: questions

Did people in the past really **have to show** their passports at every border in Europe?

Has the Channel Tunnel ever had to shut?

Why do you have to have a visa for China?

Does every tourist have to have a visa for China?

Have the police ever had to look for a bomb?

When will we have to book our flights?

Might we have to stay at home if the visas aren't ready on time?

Lies diese Sprechblasen. Die beiden markierten Teile zeigen dir, wie man Fragen mit *have to + infinitive* bildet. Finde weitere fünf Beispiele für Fragen mit *have to + infinitive* in den Sprechblasen und markiere sie.

Wenn die Verbform von *have to* aus zwei Teilen besteht (*have*[1] *had to*[2]/ *will* ______/*might* ______), kommt der erste Teil vor das Subjekt: *have the police had to...?/will we* ______ *to ...?/ might we* ______ *...?*

Besteht die ______ nur aus ______ Teil (*have*[1] *to/has to/had to*), sagt man: *do you have to ...?/*______ *every tourist have to ...?/did people* ______ *to ...?*

Sieh dir den unvollständigen Merksatz und die markierten Fragen an. Vervollständige dann den Merksatz und übertrage ihn in dein Übungsheft.

die Konjunktionen *if/when*

19 if/when

If and *when* are both conjunctions. *When* is also a question word.

1. two words in English – how many in your language?

Sieh dir an, was der Tauchlehrer sagt.

Finde die englischen Entsprechungen für 'wenn das Boot anhält', 'ein riesiger Barsch', 'vor ein paar Minuten', 'jemand fragte mich, ob...', ' die Korallen anfassen', 'denkt daran' und 'wieder auftauchen'.

Lies den Text noch einmal und trage dann die englischen Entsprechungen für die deutschen Wörter in die Tabelle rechts ein.

Übertrage die Tabelle mit je einem Beispielsatz in dein Übungsheft.

A diving lesson

When the boat stops, we'll get ready and jump into the water.

I saw a huge gouper fish **when** I dived here yesterday. I called him George.

A few minutes ago someone asked me **if** he could touch the coral.

Remember: We are visitors in this environment. **If** you just look, you won't damage any coral.

And finally: **When** must we swim back to the surface again? ...

German	English	example
als	___________	I saw ...
ob	___________	...
wann	___________	...
wenn	_____/_______	...

2. *if/when*: a problem for you?

In diesen Sätzen sind zwei Konjunkionen markiert. Welche entspricht dem Deutschen 'wenn/falls', welche entspricht 'wenn/sobald'?

If you see a beautiful fish, don't try to touch it. It might be poisonous.
We can dive for 45 minutes **if** we stay at 15 metres.

When your air is low, you must give me a signal.
Look for the anchor line of the boat **when** you go back to the surface.

Sieh dir den unvollständigen Merksatz, den Hinweis und die vier Beispielsätze an.

Vervollständige den Merksatz und übertrage ihn mit je einem Beispielsatz in dein Übungsheft.

Die englischen Konjunktionen ________ und ________ entsprechen häufig der deutschen ________________ 'wenn'.

_______ entspricht 'wenn/falls'. Es wird verwendet, wenn man sich nicht ____________ ist, ob etwas passiert (*If you see* ..., ...).

When entspricht '_________/____________'. Es wird verwendet, wenn man über einen ______________ oder eine Zeitspanne spricht (*When your air is low*, ...).

You use *if* in situations where you are not sure about something.
You use *when* in situations where you speak about a point or span of time.

3. *when* and *if* in sentences about the future

Vergleiche die Verbformen in Haupt- und Nebensatz. Was musst du in *if*- und *when-clauses* beachten, wenn du über die Zukunft sprichst? Vervollständige die Sätze.

When I see George, the grouper, I'm going to give you a sign.
George will come near you if you keep very still.

In the *main clause* you use ___________________________.

In the ____________ you use ___________________________.

~~main clause~~
a future form
a simple present form
sub-clause

20 -ing forms (1)

An *-ing* form is made with an infinitive + *ing*.

-*ing*-Formen (1)

1. -*ing* forms as a part of a verb or as a subject

Lies diesen Brief und finde heraus, weshalb Jenny sich so wohl fühlt.

Suche die englischen Entsprechungen für 'es ist ungefähr ... Grad', 'meine Schwester schwimmt (gerade)', 'seit wir angekommen sind', 'Schwimmen und Schnorcheln sind hier sehr verbreitet', 'Tauchen macht Spaß', 'ein Allradfahrzeug', 'die Straßen in der Wüste sind schnurgerade und leer' und 'Bis bald!'

Im Brief sind zwei *-ing*-Formen markiert. Finde weitere sechs und markiere sie.

Dear Sue,

Here we are in Oman. It's the end of December. I am **sitting** on the beach. The sun is shining from a clear blue sky. It's about 25 degrees. My sister is swimming. My parents are windsurfing!!!

We have been on the beach every day since we arrived. **Swimming** and snorkelling are very popular here. There are so many fish in the sea. And diving is fun, too.

Yesterday we went to the desert in a four-wheel-drive vehicle. Driving is fantastic here. The roads in the desert are so straight and empty.

See you soon.

Jenny

HINT: When the *-ing form* is a part of the verb, it is called present participle.
When the *-ing form* is the subject of a sentence, it is called gerund.

Remember:
Verb is '*Prädikat*' in German here.

Übertrage nun diese Tabelle in dein Übungsheft und ergänze sie mit den Beispielen aus dem Brief. Der Hinweis hilft dir dabei.
Markiere die *-ing*-Formen.

subject	verb	other parts
I	am **sitting**	on the beach.
The sun	is ...	...
My sister	...	...
...	...	...
Snorkelling and **swimming**	are	very popular.
Diving	...	...
...	...	

Sieh dir diesen unvollständigen Merksatz und die beiden Hinweise an.
Vervollständige dann den Merksatz und übertrage ihn in dein Übungsheft.

Eine *-ing*-Form benötigt man, um Verlaufsformen (________________ *forms*) zu bilden.

Verlaufsformen werden mit einer Form von ______ und einer ________________ gebildet. (*The sun is shining today. Yesterday it was shining, too.*)

HINT: You need an *-ing form* when you want to make a *progressive form*. Progressive forms are made with a form of *be* and an *-ing form*.

Eine *-ing*-Form kann auch ________________ eines ________________ sein. Als Subjekt wird die *-ing*-Form wie ein ________________ oder ein ________________ im Singular verwendet. (*Diving is fun. This boat is fun. It is fun.*)

HINT: An *-ing form* can also be the subject of a sentence. As a subject the *-ing form* is used like a noun or a pronoun in the singular.

Sieh dir die drei Sätze an und vergleiche die englischen und deutschen Satzbaupläne. Welche deutschen Wörter entsprechen hier der *-ing*-Form? Wo können Fehler entstehen, wenn Lernende ihre Gedanken ins Englische übertragen? Ergänze diese Sätze in deinem Übungsheft und füge die deutschen Entsprechungen hinzu.

2. *-ing* forms as subjects: are these a problem for you?

Snorkelling can be fun. — *Schnorcheln kann Spaß machen.*
Snorkelling **in Oman** can be fun. — *Im Oman zu schnorcheln …*
Snorkelling **in the warm sea** in Oman can be fun. — *Im Oman im warmen Meer …*

Snorkelling **alone** in the warm … can be fun.
Snorkelling alone **with lots of fish** in the ….
Snorkelling alone **over coral** with lots of fish ….

Lies dir den Merkvers leise vor und versuche ihn auswendig zu sagen.

3. how to write *-ing* forms

Collecting infinitives, making *-ing* forms,
And putting them in a group,
That's as easy as adding pepper to a soup.

Vergleiche die *-ing*-Formen und die Infinitive in den drei Tabellen. Welche Besonderheiten in der Schreibung stellst du fest?

infinitive + ing		
collect	–	collecting
look	–	looking
…		

infinitive (minus 'e') + ing		
make	–	making
dive	–	diving
…		

infinitive (double consonant) + ing		
put	–	putting
swim	–	…

Übertrage die Tabellen in dein Übungsheft und ergänze sie mit diesen Infinitiven sowie den dazugehörigen *-ing*-Formen.

change	ask	win	describe	clean	let	stop
arrange	drink	sit	eat	explain	shine	choose
decide	buy	count	live	get		

21 -ing forms (2)

-ing-Formen (2)

An *-ing* form can follow a verb. It can also follow a verb/noun/adjective + a preposition.

Lies die Texte und finde heraus, was die Leute davon halten, in einem tropischen Land zu leben.

1. *-ing* forms after verbs and after prepositions

Can you **imagine living** in a tropical country? Here is what five people said:

Living in hot countries

I'm not **keen on living** in a tropical country. In summer those countries get very hot. And you have a good chance of getting malaria.

I wouldn't mind living in a hot country. My parents **have talked about moving** to Sri Lanka.

There is **a high risk of getting** all kinds of illnesses. Doctors often advise having vaccinations against tropical illnesses.

Hot countries are OK. Most houses and cars have air-conditioning, so you can avoid getting too hot.

I often dream of living in a tropical country. I'm tired of living in a cold climate.

Finde die englischen Entsprechungen für 'ich bin nicht begeistert davon, in … zu leben', 'ein hohes Risiko … zu bekommen', '(sie) raten, sich gegen … impfen zu lassen' und 'ich habe es satt, in … zu leben'.

Sieh dir die markierten *-ing*-Formen und die Tabelle an. Finde weitere sechs *-ing*-Formen und markiere sie. Lege in deinem Übungsheft vier Gruppen an und ordne die Sätze mit *-ing*-Formen der richtigen Gruppe zu.

1. verb	+	-ing form	+	…			(4 sentences)
2. verb	+	preposition	+	-ing form	+	…	(2 sentences)
3. noun	+	preposition	+	-ing form	+	…	(2 sentences)
4. adjective	+	preposition	+	-ing form	+	…	(2 sentences)

2. more problems with *-ing* forms?

Would you worry about getting malaria? — ***Hättest** du **Angst**, Malaria **zu bekommen?***

Some people have a choice between living here or in a southern country. — *Einige Leute haben **die Wahl**, hier oder in einem südlichen Land **zu leben**.*

I'm looking forward to visiting our friends in Kenia. — *Ich **freue mich darauf**, unsere Freunde in Kenia **zu besuchen**.*

Sieh dir die englischen Sätze mit ihren deutschen Entsprechungen an. Achte dabei auf die deutschen Entsprechungen für die *-ing*-Formen.
Weshalb können Fehler entstehen, wenn Lernende ihre Gedanken ins Englische übertragen?

3. some expressions with *-ing* forms

Useful expressions

verb + gerund
Can you **avoid becoming** ill?
I **enjoy playing** volleyball on the beach.
We'll **finish playing** in a minute.
Imagine losing your passport!
Did you **practise writing** the words, too?
Let's **stop working** now.
Who **suggested not watching** this video?

verb + preposition + gerund
I'**m for/against taking** the train.
Are you **dreaming of lying** in the sun?
You'**ll be fined for sleeping** on the beach.
We'**re looking forward to seeing** them.
Did you **talk about flying** together?
Have you **thought of not flying** there?

adjective + preposition + gerund
I'm **afraid of flying** in small planes.
She was **bored with listening** to CDs.
Are you **good at playing** cards?
They are **known for not being punctual.**
Is he **interested in coming** with us?
He's **terrible at remembering** birthdays.

noun + preposition + gerund
I have **a terrible fear of flying.**
Did he show any **interest in helping** us?
That's **a good method of relaxing.**
What **reason** is there **for not believing** them?
They had **no intention of paying.**

Hier sind unterschiedliche Beispiele für *-ing*-Formen. Beachte in jeder Gruppe das Beispiel mit der verneinten *-ing*-Form. (Schlage die Wörter in einem Wörterbuch nach, die du nicht kennst.)

Übertrage die Beispiele als kleine *spidergrams* in dein Übungsheft.

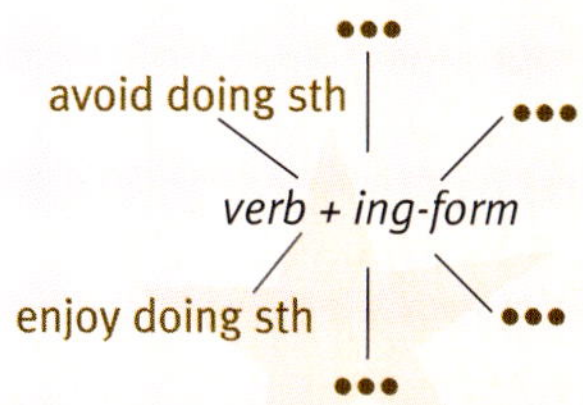

4. an exercise

1. Sue finds Scotland too wet and cold. She *doesn't like living* there.
2. David always goes by train or car. He …
3. If you have the right vaccinations, you can …
4. I've never seen the desert so I'm really … Oman.
5. Have you … a car with air-conditioning?
6. Doesn't John show any … to foreign countries?
7. I would … on the beach all day in my holidays.

a. get bored lying
b. doesn't like living
c. avoid getting ill
d. looking forward to visiting
e. interest in travelling
f. thought of renting
g. has a fear of flying

Finde die richtige Ergänzung für jeden Satz. (Die Lösung steht unten auf der Seite.)

Übertrage die Sätze in dein Übungsheft und vervollständige sie.

5. *-ing* form or *infinitive* with *to* – two different meanings

1 In Verona I **stopped** at every palace **to look** at the fantastic statues.

2 My friend has **stopped going.** She says it's too crowded.

3 I **remember asking** our guide lots of questions about the two lovers.

4 I must **remember to watch** *Romeo and Juliet* again.

a. finish one activity so you can do another
b. imagine the activity
c. think of doing an activity later
d. no longer do the activity

Hier siehst du, dass *stop* und *remember* mit *-ing*-Form oder mit Infinitiv benutzt werden können – mit unterschiedlicher Bedeutung.
Ordne die Erklärungen in der Mitte dem jeweils richtigen Satz zu. (Die Lösung findest du unten.)

1b; 2g; 3c; 4d; 5f; 6e; 7a // 1a; 2d; 3b; 4c

Langformen/ Kurzformen

22 long forms/short forms

Sieh dir diese Ansichten zum Thema 'Computerspiele' an. Finde heraus, weshalb manche Menschen sie so gern spielen.

Finde die englischen Entsprechungen für 'Was ist an diesen Spielen so spannend?', 'ich war nicht so begeistert von ...', 'man ist in einer anderen Welt ...', 'kompliziert', 'es ist nicht schwer zu ...', und 'du wirst dich überhaupt nicht langweilen'.

Im Text sind zwei *short forms* markiert. Finde weitere vierzehn und markiere sie. – Du erkennst sie an dem Apostroph (').

1. forms of *be*: past, present, future

Forms like *am*, *are* and *are not* are called long forms; *'m*, *'re* and *aren't* are called short forms.

In the mid-1990s computer games like *Doom*, *Quake* and *Alien vs. Predator* became very popular. They're known as first-person shooter games. They're still popular today. What's so exciting about these games? Why're some people worried about them? Here's what some players said: ...

First-person shooter games – dangerous or harmless?

These games are fantastic. – I wasn't so keen on the older ones because they weren't fast enough. It wasn't fun playing them.

You're in a different world when you play these games. It's cool. I'm a total fan. I like shooting my way through monsters to the next level of the game.

The graphics are super. They'll be even better in the new games. You won't be bored at all.

The stories aren't complicated. It isn't difficult to learn the rules. I'm not sure I want any new games this year.

Trage nun die acht verschiedenen Kurzformen von *be* in diese Tabelle ein. Übertrage die Tabelle zusammen mit dem Hinweis darunter in dein Übungsheft.

	positive forms		negative forms	
past:	(no short form)		________	= was not
	(no short form)		________	= were not
present:	________	= am	________	= am not
	________	= are	________	= are not
	________	= is	________	= is not
will-future:	________	= will be	________	= will not be

People often use short forms when they say or write the past, present or future forms of *be*. When you write a short form, you use an apostrophe (') where letters are missing.

Lies diesen kurzen Text und finde heraus, weshalb *first-person shooter games* vielleicht doch gefährlicher sind, als sie scheinen.

Finde dann die drei Kurzformen für *do* und trage sie in die Tabelle ein. Übertrage die Tabelle in dein Übungsheft.

2. forms of *do*: past and present

Obviously, many young people don't believe that a first-person shooter game can be dangerous. They say a game doesn't make you a killer.

However, in 1998 a fourteen-year-old boy killed three pupils and injured five others at his school in West Paducah, Kentucky, USA.

He walked into the school, didn't say a word and shot the eight people – with eight bullets. He had practised shooting with first-person shooter games, not with a real gun. Since then there have been other cases.

past:	________	= did not
present:	________	= do not
	________	= does not

3. forms of *have*: past and present

Not all computer games are violent

This is the story of a game called *Riven*. At the beginning of the game you arrive at a group of five islands. This is where Gehn lives. He's taken Catherine as his prisoner. You've got the job to find her, catch Gehn and save the islands.

You haven't got a map of the islands, but there are signs and clues that you must find.

The makers of the game have hidden many of them along paths. They've also hidden some clues in buildings. If a player hasn't chosen the right button to get into a building, the door stays shut.

The game was very popular in America. Websites appeared on the internet for players who hadn't found Catherine. Players who'd lost their way could find maps of the islands and get help online.

If you are someone who likes adventures, you'll have a lot of fun with *Riven*.

And the nice thing is that you won't have to shoot anyone!

Lies diesen Text über ein weiteres Spiel und finde heraus, wie es gespielt wird.

Finde die englischen Entsprechungen für 'seine Gefangene', 'es ist deine Aufgabe zu ...', 'eine Karte von ...', 'es gibt Wegweiser und Hinweise', 'sie haben auch ... versteckt', 'sehr beliebt', 'im Internet' und 'Spieler, die sich verirrt hatten'.

Finde neun Kurzformen im Text und markiere sie.

positive forms			**negative forms**	
past:	______	= had	______	= had not
present:	______	= have	______	= have not
	______	= has	______	= has not
future:	______	= will have	______	= will not have

Hier hast du eine unvollständige Tabelle mit Formen von *have*. Ergänze die Kurzformen von *have*.

4. other short forms

Do we need more control?

Computer games are not responsible for violent behaviour. The problem is guns. Young people shouldn't be able to buy guns.

But governments and the police can't control easily who owns, who sells and who buys guns.

If young people couldn't buy guns, we'd have fewer murders. It wouldn't be so easy to kill people.

We must do something. We mustn't wait till more people die.

______	= should not	______	= would
______	= cannot	______	= would not
______	= could not	______	= must not

Sieh dir diese Meinungen an. Finde dann die englischen Entsprechungen für 'Jugendliche sollten keine ... kaufen können', 'wir hätten weniger Morde', 'die Polizei kann nicht leicht kontrollieren, wer ...' und 'wir dürfen nicht warten, bis ...'.

Markiere die sechs Kurzformen in den Sprechblasen und trage sie in die Tabelle ein. Übertrage die Tabelle in dein Übungsheft.

they'd made = they had made; they'd make = they would make

23 may/be allowed to

May is a modal. You can find out more about modal verbs at *25 modals*.

die Verben *may/be allowed to*

Lies den Text und finde heraus, was sich an einem abgelegenen Ort in den USA 1947 ereignete.

Finde die englischen Entsprechungen für 'darf ich Ihnen ein paar Fragen stellen?', 'ein Raumfahrzeug', 'in der Wüste in der Nähe von ...', 'Leider dürfen Sie das nicht', 'Absturzstelle', und 'Weshalb durfte unser Reporter sie nicht sehen?'

Im Text findest du zusätzlich zur markierten Frage drei weitere *may*-Fragen, mit denen Ben Brown um Erlaubnis fragt. Markiere sie und die Kurzantworten dazu.

Lies den Hinweis und ergänze die Tabelle. – Übertrage sie zusammen mit dem Hinweis in dein Übungsheft.

1. asking for, giving and refusing permission

On Tuesday, July 8, 1947 Sheriff Wilcox of Roswell, New Mexico, received a phone call from Ben Brown, a journalist from Washington DC ...

"Sheriff Wilcox, **may I ask you a few questions**?"

"Yes, you may," said the sheriff.

"I believe an alien spacecraft crashed in the desert near Roswell last night," said Ben. "Local people saw something fall out of the sky. May we know what happened?"

"I'm sorry, you may not. The army is in control."

"OK. May I speak to Major Jesse Marcel?"

"I'm sorry, you can't. He's not allowed to speak to the media."

"May we speak to anybody?"

"Yes, of course you can. You can speak to me."

"Why aren't we allowed to see the site of the wreck?"

"The site is closed. The army is examining everything."

"I've heard that local residents were allowed to see the dead bodies of the four aliens. Why wasn't our reporter allowed to see them?"

"What bodies? What aliens?"

"More reporters are on their way to Roswell. When will they be allowed to go near the wreck of the UFO?"

"I'm sorry, I can't tell you. You reporters won't be allowed to see anything."

Visitors from another planet?

HINT

If you want to
- ask for permission, you can use *may*.
- give someone permission, use *may* or *can*.
- refuse permission, use *may not* or *can't*.

asking for permission with *may*		giving/refusing permission
May I ______________________	?	______________.
May we ______________________	?	______________.
______________________	?	______________.
______________________	?	______________.

2. talking about permission: past, present, future

Finde im Text oben sechs Formen von *be allowed to + infinitive* und markiere sie.

Sieh dir den unvollständigen Merksatz und den Hinweis an.
Vervollständige den Merksatz und übertrage ihn in dein Übungsheft.

Wenn man darüber sprechen möchte, ob etwas erlaubt ist, kann man ______________ + ______________ verwenden.

Für die Vergangenheit benötigt man *was*/__________/ *wasn't*/______________. Für die ______________ benötigt man *'m*/__________/*is* sowie ______________ /*aren't*/______________. Für die______________ benötigt man ______________/______________.

HINT

When you want to talk about permission in the past, present and future, you can use *be allowed to + infinitive*.
For the past you need *was/were wasn't/weren't*.
For the present you need *'m/are/is 'm not/aren't/isn't*.
For the future you need *will be/won't be*.

If you want to ask for permission, you can also use *can/could*. See *12 can*.

24 may/might

1. speculating about the past, present and future

May and *might* can both be used to talk about things that you are not sure about.

die Verben *may/might*

Sieh dir die Texte an und finde heraus, was wirklich der Fall sein könnte.

Finde die englischen Entsprechungen für 'die Armee hat vielleicht nicht die ganze Wahrheit gesagt', 'sogar heute vertuscht die Regierung vielleicht ...', 'es gibt vielleicht Photos', 'Zeitungen werden dann vielleicht die Wahrheit über ... berichten' und 'Menschen nach so vielen Jahren überzeugen'.

In den Sprechblasen sind drei Formen von *may/might* markiert.
Finde weitere zehn Formen von *may/might* und markiere sie.

One week after the crash, the US army said that the UFO was really a weather balloon. Today we still don't know very much about the crash.

The truth, the whole truth and nothing but the truth?

The army **might not have told** the whole truth in 1947. It may not have been a weather balloon that crashed in the desert. It may have been a spaceship from another planet. Some of the aliens might have survived the crash.

Even today the government **may be hiding** the facts. There may be photos and films of the aliens. Life forms from other planets might be trying to contact us. The government might know this. They might not understand some things. But we should know the truth.

One day journalists **may** finally **see the** secret documents about UFOs. Newspapers might then tell us the truth about Roswell. But people might not believe them. It may not be easy to convince people after so many years.

to speculate about ...

the past	the present	the future
may have been	______ *hiding*	*may* ______
may ______ *been*	______	______ *be*
might ______	*might be* ______	*might* ______
might ______ *told*	*might* ______	______
	______ *understand*	

Sieh dir die Tabelle und den Hinweis unten links an. Ergänze die Tabelle mit den positiven und negativen Formen aus den Texten und übertrage sie in dein Übungsheft.

You can also use *could* to speculate about the present and the future. See *12 can*.

HINT

Use these forms to speculate about
- the past:
  may/might (not) + have + past participle,
- the present:
  may/might (not) + infinitive,
  or
  may/might (not) + be + -ing form,
- the future:
  may/might (not) + infinitive.

2. an exercise

1. Ten years ago, a spacecraft with lots of aliens *... landed* in Asia.
2. These aliens *... not ... survived* on earth.
3. However, some scientists say that a few of them *... be* alive today.
4. They *... hiding* in the Himalayas.
5. Some say they *... contact* us one day.
6. Others say we *... never see* them.

Hier sind einige Sätze mit Vermutungen über die Vergangenheit, Gegenwart und Zukunft. Übertrage sie in dein Übungsheft und ergänze die Formen von *may/might*. (Die Lösung steht unten.)

1. may *or* might have landed; 2. may *or* might not have survived; 3. may be; 4. may *or* might be hiding; 5. may *or* might contact; 6. may *or* might never see

25 modals

1. the form of modal verbs

Modal verbs are a small group of verbs: Their form never changes and they are always used together with an infinitive.

Modalverben

In diesem Text kannst du herausfinden, welche Auswirkungen ein Asteroid-Aufprall haben würde.

Finde die englischen Entsprechungen für 'die meisten davon sind harmlos', 'er könnte nicht viel Schaden anrichten', 'mittelgroß', 'besonders wenn', 'er würde das Leben auf der Erde nicht zerstören', 'Würde der eine Auswirkung auf unser Leben haben?' und 'er würde viel Staub in die Atmosphäre schleudern'.

Im Text sind vier Subjekte und Prädikate mit *could* markiert. Finde weitere zehn Beispiele mit *could* bzw. *would* im Text und markiere sie.

Asteroids – a danger to life on earth?

Millions of asteroids are flying through space. Many of them come close to earth, some hit earth. Most of these are harmless. But **some asteroids could be** dangerous.

A small asteroid could land in your garden or on top of your car. **It couldn't cause** much damage, but it could make a big hole in the ground.

A medium-sized asteroid would cause more damage, especially if it landed in a town or city. But it wouldn't destroy life on earth.

And what about a large asteroid? Would that have an effect on our life? Could it be a danger to life on earth? **Why could it destroy** life?

A very large asteroid – perhaps five kilometres wide – could kill all life on earth. It would throw a lot of dust into the atmosphere. The light from the sun wouldn't reach the earth for a very long time. Temperatures would fall, and that would mean the end of life on earth.

Hier hast du eine tabellarische Übersicht über die Verwendung von Modalverben. Übertrage die Tabellen in dein Übungsheft und ergänze sie mit je drei Beispielen.

	subject	verb: modal	verb: infinitive	other parts
positive statements:	Some asteroids	could	be	dangerous.
	A small asteroid	would	cause	…
	…			
negative statements:	It	couldn't	cause	…
	…	wouldn't	destroy	

	question word	modal	subject	infinitive	other parts
questions:	Why	could	it	destroy	life?
		Could	…	…	…?

Sieh dir den unvollständigen Merksatz und den Hinweis an. Vervollständige den Merksatz und übertrage ihn zusammen mit den *modals* in dem Kasten in dein Übungsheft.

! Die ____________ eines *modal* ändert sich ____________.

____________ einem *modal* verwendet man einen ____________________.

In ____________________ Sätzen verwendet man *n't* (oder *not*) ______________ dem *modal*.

In ______________ steht das *modal* ________ dem Subjekt, der Infinitiv ____________ dem Subjekt.

some more modals:

can	*can't*
may	*may not*
might	*might not*
must	*mustn't*
should	*shouldn't*

HINT

- The form of a modal never changes:
  They could land. It could land.
- After a modal you use an infinitive:
  It could kill. It wouldn't reach ….
- For negative statements you add *n't* (or *not*) after the modal:
  It couldn't cause …
  It wouldn't destroy …
- In questions the word order is modal + subject + infinitive + …:
  Why could it destroy …?
  Could it be …?

2. the function of modals: expressing how certain something is

Lies diese Sätze und finde die englischen Entsprechungen für 'in der Nähe meiner Heimatstadt', 'bevor Wissenschafter es verhindern können', 'Wasser bedeckt ungefähr ...', 'die Erdoberfläche' und 'mindestens ein Asteroid, der die Erde trifft ...'.

1 One day an asteroid **might** land near my home town.

2 A big asteroid **may** crash into earth before scientists can stop it.

3 Our planet **could** be destroyed, but not during my life.

4 Most asteroids **should** come down in the sea. Water covers about 70% of the earth's surface.

5 At least one asteroid that hits the earth **must** crash on land. About 30% of the earth's surface is land.

Sieh dir die Sätze und diese Tabelle an. Trage die restlichen vier Modalverben an der richtigen Stelle ein. (Die Lösung steht unten auf der Seite.)

very uncertain		almost certain	certain
might, ________,	________	________	________

For more about modals see:
12 can/could
18 have to
24 may/might

an exercise

- To talk about the past, use *have + modal + past participle*:
  It might have hit ...
  It must have changed ...
- To talk about the present, use a *modal + infinitive*.
- To talk about the future, use a *modal + infinitive*.
  We might be ...
  We should give ...

give – change – do – be – kill – use – have – ~~hit~~ – be

Some scientists say that ...

1. about 64 million years ago a large asteroid *may have hit* the earth. After the crash, the climate *must ...* and that *could ...* all the dinosaurs.
2. we *might ...* in the middle of a climate change now. Winters in Europe *should ...* much colder. Countries in Asia and Africa *shouldn't ...* so many floods and tornados every year.
3. we *could ...* much more for the environment now and in the future. We *must ...* more alternative forms of energy. We *should ...* our children a chance to live better lives.

Finde für jeden Satz das richtige Verb und die richtige Form. Der Hinweis hilft dir dabei. Übertrage die Sätze in dein Übungsheft und ergänze sie. (Die Lösung steht unten auf der Seite.)

Füge den Hinweis und die Tabelle oben hinzu.

3. the function of modals: expressing how free someone is

You can use modals to say how free a person is or what duties a person has.

totally free → unfree
can — *should* — *must*

How free or unfree are scientists?

1. I think scientists are free people. If they want to, they ... inform people about possible dangers.
2. But they sometimes have a dilemma: They ... tell the truth, but that's bad for their companies.
3. People are more important than a company. They ... inform us – even if they lose their jobs.

What duties does the public have?

1. We are a free country. The public ... get all the information they want.
2. Not just that. People ... inform themselves. I think it's their duty.
3. But there are people who think we ... not know everything because that might lead to a panic.

Hier hast du eine Grafik und unterschiedliche Meinungen: Wie frei sind Wissenschaftler? Welche Verpflichtungen hat die Allgemeinheit?

Finde die englischen Entsprechungen für 'mögliche Gefahren', 'selbst wenn', 'nicht nur das' und 'weil das eine Panik auslösen könnte'.

Übertrage den Text in dein Übungsheft und ergänze ihn. (Die Lösung steht unten.) Füge die Grafik hinzu.

very uncertain: might, may, could; almost certain: should; certain: must //
1. may have hit, must have changed, could have killed; 2. might be, should be, shouldn't have; 3. could do, must use, should give //
1. can; 2. should; 3. must; 4. can; 5. must; 6. should

die Verben *must/have to* (müssen)

Lies diese drei Kurztexte und finde die englischen Entsprechungen für 'wieder einmal müssen wir Vögel retten', 'tausende Vögel mussten sterben', 'die Küstenwache', 'Lotsen mussten ihr Leben riskieren' und 'in Zukunft müssen sie sich genauer an Anweisungen halten'.

Im Text sind drei Subjekte und Verbformen markiert. Finde vier weitere Formen von *have to* und zwei Formen von *must* und markiere sie.

Remember:
You use *had to*, *must* and *will have to* for all persons.

Übertrage diese Tabelle in dein Übungsheft und ergänze sie mit den Beispielen aus den Texten.

Sieh dir die Beispiele für Fragen an und finde die englischen Entsprechungen für 'Musste dieser Unfall passieren?', 'solche riesigen Tanker', 'Warum müssen wir bezahlen ...?', 'wild lebende Tiere und Pflanzen' und 'Wie lange müssen wir ... hinnehmen?'

Sieh dir den unvollständigen Merksatz und die Beispiele an.
Vervollständige den Merksatz und übertrage ihn in dein Übungsheft.

26 must/have to

The verb *must* is a modal. You can use it to talk about the present. You use *had to* for the past and *will have to* for the future.

1. positive statements

Supertankers – a danger to wildlife

Another oil tanker has sunk near the coast, and the sea has washed oil onto the beaches. Once again **we must rescue** birds and clean the beaches.

Last year **thousands of birds had to die** after a tanker accident. Now thousands more must die. **These accidents will have to stop.**

The coastguard had to rescue the crew of the tanker. Pilots had to risk their lives in very bad weather. Captains of tankers must understand that the coast is dangerous. In future they will have to follow instructions more carefully. Companies will have to make sure their ships are safe.

Normally you pronounce *must* as [məst].

must* and *have to

the past	the present	the future
thousands of birds had to die	*we must ...*	*these accidents ...*
...	...	...

2. questions with *must*, *had to*, *will have to*

Did this accident have to happen? Why did the coastguard have to rescue the crew?

Will more tankers have to sink before the situation improves? How long will we have to accept this situation?

Must companies use such huge tankers to transport oil? **Why must we pay to clean** the beaches and save all the wildlife?

Der Satzbauplan für Fragen über ...

- die **Vergangenheit** ist: ________ + subject + *have to* + infinitive ...?

  Beispiel: *Did this* ______________________________?

- die **Gegenwart** ist: ________ + subject + infinitive ...?

  Beispiel: *Why* ______________________________?

- die **Zukunft** ist: ________ + ________ + *have to* + ________ ...?

  Beispiel: *How long* ______________________________?

3. negative statements with *must* and *have to:* a problem for you?

Sieh dir den Leserbrief und die Sprechblasen an und finde heraus, was der Verfasser und ein Helfer zu sagen haben.

Finde die englischen Entsprechungen für 'sie müssen strengere Gesetze machen', 'sie dürfen ohne Lotsen nicht in gefährlichen Gewässern fahren', 'sie dürfen nicht unvorsichtig sein', 'wir mussten/brauchten die Leute nicht fragen', 'man muss/braucht kein Experte sein' und 'du musst/brauchst morgen nicht zu helfen'.

Im Text sind zwei Formen markiert. Finde zwei weitere Formen von *mustn't* + *infinitive* sowie vier verneinte Formen von *have to* + *infinitive* und markiere sie.

A letter to the editor

Dear Sir or Madam,

We have had enough. These accidents must stop. Governments must talk to the oil companies. And they must make stricter laws:

1. **Supertankers mustn't come** close to the coast.
2. They mustn't sail in dangerous waters without a pilot.
3. Captains of supertankers mustn't be so careless, especially in stormy weather.

Yours faithfully,

Hugh Hanley,
Aylesbury
h.hanley@shines.net

After the accident

You won't have to help tomorrow. We have enough people.

A sick bird doesn't have to suffer if we can clean it quickly.

You don't have to be an expert if you want to help. Volunteers don't have to work every day.

We didn't have to ask people for help after the accident. They saw the photos of the birds and they wanted to help.

HINT

- You use the negative form *mustn't* to say that somebody is not allowed to do something. It is pronounced ['mʌsnt].
- You use the negative forms of *have to* when you want to say that it is not necessary to do something, but you can do it.
  For the past you use *didn't have to*, for the present *don't/doesn't have to* and for the future *won't have to.*

Sieh dir diesen Hinweis und den unvollständigen Merksatz an.

Ergänze dann den Merksatz zur Verwendung von *mustn't* und den verneinten Formen von *have to* und übertrage ihn in dein Übungsheft.

Die verneinte ______________ *mustn't* wird verwendet um ausdrücken, dass jemand etwas auf keinen Fall tun ____________ oder tun sollte. (*Captains* ________________ *be careless.*)

Um auszudrücken, dass es _____________ nötig ist etwas zu tun, dass man es aber tun __________, werden die __________________ Formen von *have to* verwendet: Die _____________________ wird mit *didn't have to*, die ___________________ mit *don't/doesn't have to* und die Zukunft mit _______________________ gebildet.

4. an exercise

Sieh dir die Satzanfänge und Satzenden an. Kombiniere sie so, dass du fünf sinnvolle Sätze erhältst. (Die Lösung steht unter der Übung.) Übertrage die Sätze in dein Übungsheft.

1. You mustn't walk along the rocks,
2. You don't have to help now,
3. You didn't have to help
4. You mustn't go into the sea,
5. You mustn't touch these birds,

a. the tide is going out.
b. they've been dead for two days.
c. they're full of oil.
d. if you didn't want to.
e. we've nearly finished.

1c; 2e; 3d; 4a; 5b

verneinte Aussagesätze

Sieh dir die Überschrift und die Sprechblasen an. Finde heraus, welche Gerüchte der Präsident dementiert.

Finde die englischen Entsprechungen für 'Gerüchte und Dementi', 'sie ist nicht mit mir nach ... gereist', 'wir telefonieren nicht heimlich', 'die Zeitungen berichten nicht die Wahrheit', 'wir lassen uns nicht scheiden', '(sie) arbeitet seit zwei Jahren in meinem Büro', 'ich werde nicht ruhen bis ...' und 'sie dürfen auf solche Lügen nicht hören'.

In den Sprechblasen sind Subjekte und Formen des *simple past, present perfect, present progressive, simple present* sowie Futur- und Modalformen markiert. Lies den Hinweis oben rechts und markiere dann die restlichen elf Subjekte mit verneinten Prädikaten.

27 negative statements

It is quite easy to make negative statements in English: You add the short form ...*n't* to an auxiliary or you put *not* behind an auxiliary.

1. finding the forms

Sieh dir nun die Sprechblasen und diese sechs Aussagen über verschiedene Zeiten an. Ordne die Sprechblasen den Aussagen zu. (Die Lösung steht unten.)

2. organizing the forms: a checklist about different times

the past	from the past to the present	the present (*now, at the moment*)	the future
☐	☐	☐	☐ and ☐

with modals ☐

about permanent situations, regular events and actions (*often, regularly, every ...*) ☐

about the past: 1; the time from the past to the present: 5; the present: 3; the future: 4 and 7; for a permanent situation/things that happen all the time: 2; with modals: 6

to talk about the past:

She didn't ______________________________.

to talk about the time from ____________ to ______________:

Miss Tomkins hasn't ______________________________.

to talk about the ______________:

The newspapers __________ *telling* ______________________.

to talk about ______________ with 'will':

They ____________ *ever* ________________ *stories again.*

to talk about the______________ with 'going to':

My wife ______________________________ *leave me.*

to talk about ______________, regular events, __________:

______________________________.

with modals:

______________________________.

3. how to make negative statements

Sieh dir diese unvollständige Tabelle, die Sprechblasen und die Checkliste auf Seite 48 an und vervollständige die Tabelle.

Übertrage die Tabelle dann in dein Übungsheft und füge je einen weiteren Beispielsatz aus den Sprechblasen hinzu.

– Für ______________ Aussagen über **die Vergangenheit** braucht man nur__________ Form: *didn't* + ______________.

– Für die Zeit **von der** ______________ **bis zur Gegenwart** gibt es __________ Formen: __________ + *past participle* **oder** *hasn't* + ______________. Für *he, she, it* verwendet man __________ *(Miss Tomkins* __________ *sold her story).*

– Um über **die Gegenwart** zu sprechen, braucht man eine verneinte __________ von *be* + ______________ *participle (I'm not lying to you; she* __________ *answering any questions; they* ______________ *telling the truth).*

– Für **die** __________ verwendet man *won't* + __________ *(I* ________ *rest till I know who invented these stories)* **oder** eine verneinte __________ von *be* + *going to* + __________ *(I'm* ________ *going to marry Miss Tomkins; my wife and I* ______________________ *get divorced).*

– Für **Dauerzustände** und für **Dinge, die** ______________ geschehen, braucht man __________ oder *doesn't* + ______________. __________ steht nach *he, she* und *it (Miss Tomkins* __________ *visit me privately).*

– Nach **verneinten Modalverben** steht ein ______________ *(You can't/ shouldn't/mustn't believe this).*

Sieh dir diesen Merksatz zur Verwendung des *simple past, present perfect, present progressive,* der Futurformen, der Modalverben und des *simple present* zusammen mit dem Hinweis und den Sprechblasen an.

Vervollständige den Merksatz und übertrage ihn zusammen mit dem Hinweis in dein Übungsheft.

HINT

- infinitives: *work, give, tell*
- present participles: *working, giving, telling*
- past participles: *worked, given, told*
- negative forms of *be*: *'m not, aren't, isn't*

- For negatives with *be* as a main verb, look at pages 20–23.
- For negatives with *do* as a main verb, look at pages 28–29.
- For negatives with *have* as a main verb, look at pages 30–31.
- For more information also look at the entries for *can, have to, may, modals* and *must.*

Nomen/Substantive (1)

Sieh dir den Text an und knobele die fehlenden Buchstaben in der verschlüsselten Nachricht heraus.

Finde die englischen Entsprechungen für 'eine Flaschenpost', 'verschlüsselte Nachricht', '(es) war ihm ein Rätsel', 'er hatte viele Geheimcodes geknackt', 'ein Textverarbeitungsprogramm' und 'der Schlüssel zu dem Code'.

For more about *letters and sounds*, see *8 the alphabet*.

Sieh dir den unvollständigen Merksatz und die Hinweise an. Vervollständige dann den Merksatz und übertrage ihn in dein Übungsheft.

Sieh dir nun die Checkliste und die zwei Tabellen rechts an. Übertrage die Tabellen in dein Übungsheft und ordne dann die Nomen in dem Kasten jeweils der richtigen Gruppe zu.

If you don't know some of the nouns, look them up in a dictionary.

28 nouns (1): introduction

Nouns are the largest word class. They are the 'names' we give to people, things, places, feelings, etc.

1. spelling

A message in a bottle

Detective Grammar looked at the message. He had found it in a bottle in a box on the beach. Detective Grammar loved empty beaches, but this beach was full of bottles and boxes. He looked at the coded message again. The code was a mystery to him:

✌●❍□⬧♦ ♋●● ■□◆■⬧ ⤤□❒❍ ♦♒♏♓❒ □●◆❒♋●⬧ ⬧♓♦♒ '–⬧'.

Detective Grammar had cracked many secret codes and solved many mysteries before. Not just in this country. He had been to many countries, to England, France, Germany. He had decoded messages in English, French, German and in other languages. There were eight words. What were they? Articles, adjectives, nouns? Or were they pronouns and prepositions? There were 5 dots. Was each dot one letter?

Suddenly Grammar remembered. He had seen these symbols before. Could they be from a font in a word processing program? He went back to his hotel. He didn't have his laptop, so he asked for one of their laptops. He checked the fonts. Soon he found the key to the code and wrote down these letters.

A l m o s t a _ _ n _ u _ _ f _ r _

_ h e i _ p _ _ _ _ _ _ w _ _ _ '–_'.

- ______ werden im Englischen ______ geschrieben (z.B. *message*, ______).
  - Ausnahmen sind Namen (*Detective Grammar*, ______, ______) und der ______ eines Satzes.

You use a capital letter for all names and at the beginning of a sentence.

2. singular/plural (1)

checklist:
Does the noun end with …?
- a voiced consonant (b, d, g, etc.)
- a voiced consonant + e
- a vowel sound [-iː, -ə, …]

or:
- a voiceless consonant (p, t, k, etc.)
- a voiceless consonant + e

Add *–s*, say [-z].		
words	codes	trees
…	…	…
…	…	…

Add *–s*, say [-s].	
notebooks	notes
…	…

fingerprints • criminals • detectives • laws • computers • clues • fonts • gangs • laptops • websites • prisons • guides • lawyers • dots • crimes • secret agents • word processing programs • courts • adventures • inspectors • bodyguards

3. singular/plural (2)

Checklist: Does the noun end with …?

–ce, –se, –ge, –ze **or** –s, –x, –ch, –sh

buses • bushes • languages • exercises • foxes • garages • beaches
prizes • watches • secret services • witnesses • sentences • offences
searches • glasses • homepages

Add –*s*, say [-ɪz].			**Add –*es*, say [-ɪz].**		
message	–	*messages*	box	–	*boxes*
language	–	________	beach	–	________
…	–	…	…	–	…

Sieh dir die Checkliste, den Kasten mit Nomen und die Tabelle an.
Finde die beiden fehlenden Pluralformen in dem Kasten und trage sie ein.
Übe die Aussprache der Plurale mit der Endung [-ɪz].

Übertrage dann die Tabelle in dein Übungsheft und ordne die Nomen aus dem Kasten mit Singular und Plural zu.

4. singular/plural (3)

- Nouns with the ending vowel + *-y* have the plural ending *-ys*.
- Nouns with the ending consonant + *-y* have the plural ending *-ies*.

boy	–	*boys*	country	–	________
key	–	________	mystery	–	________
…	–	…	…	–	…

activities • ceremonies • toys • ladies • secretaries
keys • universities • valleys • societies • families
ways • countries • minorities • cities • robberies
days • chimneys • mysteries

Lies den Hinweis, die Tabelle und den Kasten mit Nomen.
Finde die drei fehlenden Plurale in dem Kasten und trage sie ein.
Übertrage dann die Tabelle in dein Übungsheft und ordne die Nomen aus dem Kasten mit Singular und Plural zu.

5. singular/plural (4)

cat	–	________	horse	–	________	girl	–	________
mouse	–	________	sheep	–	________	woman	–	________
knife	–	________	cake	–	________	husband	–	________
fork	–	________	loaf	–	________	wife	–	________
life	–	________	detective	–	________	flower	–	________
death	–	________	thief	–	________	leaf	–	________
						a German	–	________
						a Japanese	–	________

women • knives • lives • thieves • mice • loaves
sheep • leaves • wives • two Japanese

Jedes dieser Wortpaare hat eine regelmäßige bzw. unregelmäßige Pluralform.

Finde die unregelmäßigen Formen in dem Kasten unten und trage sie ein.
Ergänze dann die regelmäßigen Formen.
Übertrage die Liste in dein Übungsheft.

6. singular/plural (5)

Singular
tooth • man
person • hovercraft
fish • scarf • child
half • foot • grapefruit

Plural
halves • fish
men • people
children • teeth • grapefruit
scarves • hovercraft • feet

Ordne diese Singularformen ihren unregelmäßigen Pluralformen zu und übertrage sie in einer Tabelle in dein Übungsheft.

Regular plurals:
roof – roofs
chef – chefs
chief – chiefs
safe – safes

29 nouns (2): countable & uncountable

Nomen/Substantive (2)

Sieh dir das Bild und den Text an und finde heraus, weshalb Emma erst nach zwei Uhr zu Mittag isst.

Finde die englischen Entsprechungen für 'Emma ist in einem Bistro angestellt', 'die Bistros füllen sich', ' einige Leute ... andere Leute ...' und 'eine Kollegin/ein Kollege'.

Im Text sind vier Nomen mit Begleitern markiert. Finde im Text weitere zwanzig Nomen – teils mit, teils ohne Begleiter – und markiere sie. (Die Lösung steht unten auf der Seite.)

Sieh dir die Tabelle zum Gebrauch der *countable nouns* an und ordne jeder Regel eines der Beispiele rechts zu. (Die Lösung steht unten auf der Seite.)

Übertrage die Tabelle mit den Beispielen in dein Übungsheft.

1. countable nouns

Most English nouns can be put into two groups: *countable nouns* and *uncountable nouns*. Almost all English nouns are *countable nouns*.

Emma works in **a bistro** in **the city centre**. **Every day** at 12 o'clock **the bistros** and the cafés become very busy. This part of the town has many offices.

Lots of people want sandwiches, baguettes and hot and cold drinks.

Some people sit down, eat a sandwich or drink a cappucino or an espresso. Other people buy three or four sandwiches for their friends or for a colleague in the office.

At two o'clock the bistro is quiet again and Emma can eat her lunch. She likes these quiet periods.

1. **Countable nouns** have a singular and a plural form.
2. Before **singular forms** you **must** use ...
   - 2.1 an indefinite article (*a/an*)
   - 2.2 a definite article (*the*)
   - 2.3 a possessive determiner (*my, ...*)
   - 2.4 *one, each, every, another*
   - 2.5 *this/that.*
3. **Plural forms can** be used after ...
   - 3.1 a definite article (*the*)
   - 3.2 numbers (*two, three, ...*)
   - 3.3 possessive determiners (*my, ...*)
   - 3.4 quantifiers (*a few, some, ...*)
   - 3.5 *these/those.*
4. They can be used on their own.

Examples:

a. her lunch
b. baguettes
c. the bistros
d. three or four sandwiches
e. this part
f. their friends
g. every day
h. a sandwich/sandwiches
i. lots of people
j. a colleague/an espresso
k. these quiet periods
l. the office

2. uncountable nouns and countable nouns

Sieh dir die Sätze mit dem *uncountable noun 'work'* und dem *countable noun 'job' an.*

Finde die englischen Entsprechungen für 'Arbeit wie Emmas kann anstrengend sein', 'eine Stelle wie Emmas ...', 'manche Arbeit ist gut bezahlt', 'manche Stellen sind ...', 'die Arbeit, die ungelernte Arbeitskräfte tun können, ...'.

Sieh dir die Sätze und den unvollständigen Merksatz mit dem Hinweis auf Seite 53 an.

Work like Emma's can be stressful.	**A job** like Emma's can be stressful.
She is lucky that she has found **work.**	Emma's friends haven't found **jobs.**
Some work is well paid in her town.	**Some jobs are** well paid in her town.
A lot of work seems to be low paid.	**A lot of jobs seem** to be low paid.
However, **most of this work is** for highly-skilled people.	**Most of these jobs are** for highly-skilled people.
There isn't much work for unskilled people.	**There aren't many jobs** for unskilled people.
Obviously, **the work that unskilled workers can do** is low paid.	Obviously, **the jobs that unskilled workers can do** are low paid.

the cafés; this part; the town; many offices; lots of people; sandwiches; baguettes; drinks; some people; a sandwich; a cappucino; an espresso; other people; three or four sandwiches; their friends; a colleague; the office; the bistro; her lunch; these quiet periods

1 h; 2.1 j; 2.2 l; 2.3 a; 2.4 g; 2.5 e; 3.1 c; 3.2 d; 3.3 f; 3.4 i; 3.5 k; 4 b;

Im Gegensatz zu *countable nouns* (*job*/*jobs*), haben *uncountable nouns* (*work*) nur _________ Form. Diese Form kann __________ Artikel verwendet werden (*Work like Emma's …*). Nur wenn von etwas Bestimmtem gesprochen wird, darf ein ___________________ benutzt werden (*the work that unskilled people can do …*).
Uncountable nouns werden mit einer Verbform im ________________ verbunden, selbst wenn sie mit Mengenangaben verwendet werden (*this work* _______, *some work* _______, *a lot of work* ____________, *there* ____________ *much work*).

HINT

Uncountable nouns …
- have one form
- are normally used without an article
- are used with an article when you speak about something in particular
- are used with a singular verb form, even after the quantifiers *some*, *a lot of*.

Ergänze den Merksatz und übertrage ihn in dein Übungsheft.

3. uncountable nouns with and without *the*

TO ALL OUR GUESTS:
We know that our guests **want information about** their food.
Our waiters are able to **give advice** at all times. We train them to **give the information that our guests want.** Ask them and they will **give you all the advice you need.**
We know that **quality is important** for our guests. Experience **the quality of our cooking.**
Test our service.

Wenn man über etwas im Allgemeinen spricht, verwendet man *uncountable nouns* ____________ Artikel (*want information about*, ________________ *is important*).
Wenn man über etwas Bestimmtes spricht, verwendet man *uncountable nouns* __________ Artikel (_____________________ *that our guests want*, _______________________ *of our cooking*).

Sieh dir den Text links an und finde heraus, wie hier Gäste geworben werden sollen.
Achte dabei darauf, wie die *uncountable nouns* *'information'*, *'advice'* und *'quality'* mit und ohne Artikel verwendet werden.

Lies dann den unvollständigen Merksatz und vervollständige ihn. Übertrage ihn in dein Übungsheft.

4. some more uncountable nouns

Useful words

substances: cement, sand, coal, paper, wool, iron, gold, silver, pasta, rice, bread, sugar, fish, chicken, meat, pork
liquids: water, milk, juice, coffee
abstract ideas: love, hate, peace, time, progress, knowledge

school subjects: economics, ethics, genetics, mathematics
activities: aerobics, athletics, gymnastics
games: billiards, darts, cards
others: information, advice, luggage, furniture, news, homework

Beachte:
Die blauen Wörter werden im Deutschen oft im Plural verwendet. Im Englischen ist das nicht möglich.
Die roten Wörter sehen wie Pluralformen aus, müssen aber mit einer Verbform im Singular verwendet werden.

5. making uncountable nouns countable

pasta	a kilo of	bread
rice	a spoonful of	pork
sugar		meat
	a slice of	ham
fish		
chicken	a piece of	water
meat		milk
information	a bottle of	juice
advice	a glass of	coffee
furniture	a cup of	tea
luggage	a litre of	petrol

Die Sprechblasen links zeigen, wie *uncountable nouns* zu *'countables'* gemacht werden können.
Lege in deinem Übungsheft eine Liste an, in der du *phrases* aus der mittleren Spalte mit den Nomen verbindest. – Die Farbmarkierung zeigt, was zusammengehört.

30 nouns (3): more about nouns

Nomen/Substantive (3)

Sieh dir die Überschrift und Amys E-Mail an und finde heraus, was ihr ein bisschen peinlich war.

Finde die englischen Entsprechungen für 'Seniorenausflug', 'die Musik von Tom Jones', '(sie) bestand darauf, dass ich mit ihr ginge', 'das Durchschnittsalter der Fans', '(er) war eigentlich ganz gut', 'die Stimmen der SängerInnen', 'ein bisschen peinlich' und 'bis bald'.

In der E-Mail sind zwei Stellen markiert.
Finde weitere sieben solcher 'Wortpaare' und markiere sie.

1. Watch the apostrophe: ...'s and ...s'

Old-timers' outing

From: amy@welshweb.co.uk
(amy watson)
To: markus@germannet.de

Hi Markus,
Do you remember how I said my mum loves **Tom Jones's music**? Well, last week **Tom Jones** was in Cardiff.
It was Mum's birthday, so I bought her a ticket. Mum was thrilled and insisted I went with her. Then her friend Barbara decided to come.
Next, Barbara's friend Jenny wanted to come, too. So I had mum, her friend and her friend's friend all in the car.
When we got to the concert, I nearly died. The fans were all old-timers. I'm sure the fans' average age was 60. Mum and her friends were the youngest people there.
Tom Jones was actually quite good. He had fantastic singers and dancers. I really liked the singers' voices.
Fortunately, Mum didn't behave like a silly teenager. Her friends' behaviour was a bit embarrassing, but they said they were only joking. I hope they were.

C u soon.
*Amy***

Lege dir in deinem Übungsheft zwei Listen (...*'s* und ...*s'*) an und ergänze sie mit den Beispielen aus der E-Mail.

...'s	
Tom Jones	Tom Jones's music
Mum	...

...s'	
old-timers	an old-timers' outing
the fans	...

HINT

You write ...
– *'s* after a singular noun:
Tom Jones's music, Mum's car
– *s'* for almost all plural nouns:
the singers' voices,
the fans' average age
– *'s* after irregular plural forms:
people's opinions, the children's toys
women's rights, men's work.
For the pronunciation of the endings see **28 nouns (1)**.

Sieh dir den unvollständigen Merksatz, den Hinweis rechts sowie deine beiden Listen an.
Ergänze den Merksatz und übertrage ihn zusammen mit der Sprechblase unten rechts in dein Übungsheft.

Du schreibst ...

- *'s* nach einem ____________ im Singular (____________________________, ____________________________) und nach unregelmäßigen ____________________ (________________________, ____________________).
- *s'* nach einem Nomen im ________________ (____________________________, ____________________________).

Useful phrases

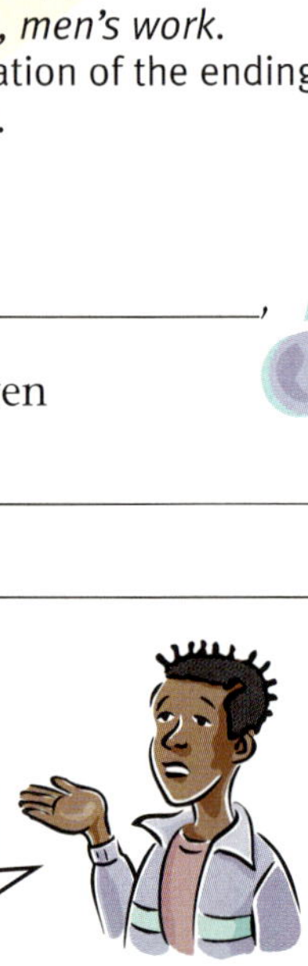

You don't always have to repeat the whole phrase:
Is that your Tom Jones CD?
– No, it's Mum's.

Übertrage diese *phrases* in dein Übungsheft. Schlage in einem Wörterbuch nach, was du nicht verstehst.

my dog's name	the EU's population	a day's journey
my cat's basket	London's museums	tomorrow's weather
the Earth's atmosphere	the city's one-way system	in a week's/month's time
America's wildlife	today's TV programme	in three weeks' time
		in a few months' time

2. talking about 'possession' with …'s, …s' and … of …

Lies diese Sätze und finde die englischen Entsprechungen für 'die Musik der Corrs', 'eine Besprechung ihrer letzten CD', 'ein Inserat/eine Anzeige', 'der Veranstaltungsort für …' und 'jemand hatte die Idee'.

1 **Amy's favourite group** is the Corrs. She listens to **the Corrs' music** a lot.

2 The venue for **next month's concert** will be **the city's new concert hall.**

3 It was **someone's idea** to use my car, but I don't want to drive to Cardiff again.

4 She read **a review of their latest CD** in the paper yesterday. There was also an ad with **the dates of their next tour.**

5 **My parrot's favourite group** is Metallica.

Sieh dir die markierten Teile in den Sprechblasen und diese Regeln über 'Besitz' an. Trage dann die Zahlen der Sprechblasen ein. (Die Lösung steht unten auf der Seite.) Übertrage die Regeln und die Sprechblase links in dein Übungsheft.

- You use …'s and …s' to talk about 'possession' with …

people	☐	time and place	☐
indefinite pronouns	☐	pets/animals	☐

- You use '… *of* …' to talk about 'possession' with things. ☐

Sometimes you use ***of*** and ***'s***: *Tom is a friend of Amy's (that is, one of Amy's friends).*

3. gender: nouns and personal pronouns (subject and object form)

Sieh dir die Nomen auf den Zetteln und die Sprechblase mit Personalpronomen an. Ordne jedem Zettel zwei der Pronomen zu. (Die Lösung steht unten auf der Seite.)

Vergleiche die englischen Pronomen für diese Nomen mit den deutschen Entsprechungen. Bei welchen der Nomen, denkst du, haben Lernende gelegentlich Probleme mit der Wahl des Personalpronomens?

they him ? he she it it her them

1 Amy / a woman / my friend Joan / our cousin Nicola
subject: ________ object: ________

2 Tom / a man / my friend Markus / our cousin Nick
subject: ________ object: ________

3 his concert / her review / your ticket / our outing
subject: ________ object: ________

4 women / men / friends / cousins / concerts / tickets / prices / guitars
subject: ________ object: ________

4. a problem for you?

HINT Sometimes you can't tell from a noun if it is used for a male or a female person *(friend, cousin, etc)*. You can often only tell from a name, the personal pronoun or from the context if the noun is used for a woman or a man *(friend – Amy – she; friend – Tom – he)*.

You'll meet a colleague of mine at the concert.
Amy is also a good friend. ________ was a young teacher when I first met ________. Now ________ is a headteacher.
I was introduced to ______ by one of my cousins.
You know, the one who is a police officer. ________ introduced ________ to me many years ago.

Lies den Hinweis und ergänze dann den Lückentext mit Personalpronomen. Verwende dann *Tom* als Name und übertrage den Text in dein Übungsheft. Wie wirkt sich der Name auf die Personalpronomen aus? Wie verändern sich die deutschen Entsprechungen für die markierten Wörter?

1 she, her; 2 he, him; 3 it, it; 4 they, them
people: 1; indefinite pronouns: 4; time and place: 3; animals: 5; things: 2 //

Zahlen

Sieh dir das Bild und den Text an und finde heraus, worum es in diesem Telefongespräch geht.

Finde die englischen Entsprechungen für 'eine Einwohnerzahl von etwa ...', 'man braucht weniger als ... mit dem Zug', 'mit dem Auto fährt man am besten auf der ...', 'ein Fax schicken, um die Buchung zu bestätigen', 'die Vorwahl für', 'die Postleitzahl' und 'eins Komma zwei'.

31 numbers

1. what you may hear ... and what you may see written down

... Torquay has a population of about **one hundred and fifteen thousand**[1]. It's about **two hundred and twenty miles**[2] from London ...

... It takes less than **three and a half hours**[3] by train. A ticket costs **forty-five pounds fifty**[4] ...

... By car it's best to take **the M four** and **the M five**, and then follow **the A three, eight, oh**[5] from Exeter ...

From a telephone conversation

... You can send a fax to confirm the booking. The code for Britain is **double oh, double four**[6]. The code for Torquay is **one, eight, oh, three**[7]. And our number is **three, two, five, three, seven, eight**[8] ...

... You can also send a letter. Our address is **twenty-seven Brim Hill**[9], Torquay. The post code is **TQ one, four TR**[10]. It's exactly **one point two kilometres**[11] from our house to the beach ... .

For more about **numbers**, see *14 the date* and *52 the time.*

Ordne nun die 'gehörten' Zahlen diesen Schreibungen zu.

a 0044 *6*	b 1.2 km	c M4, M5, A380	d 27 Brim Hill
e TQ1 4TR	f 220 m	g 3 1/2 hrs	h 325378
i 115,000	j 1803	k £ 45.50	

2. what you may see... – ... and what you can say

Lege in deinem Übungsheft eine Tabelle an, in der du einträgst, wie du bestimmte Zahlen sagen kannst. (Wichtige Unterschiede zum Deutschen findest du in dem Hinweis rechts. Markiere sie in deinem Übungsheft.)

- **telephone numbers**:
  0044 – *double oh, double four*
  1803 – *one, ...*
- **post codes**:
  TQ1 4TR – *TQ one ... TR*
- **house numbers**:
  ... Brim Hill – ...
- **distances**: ...
- **road numbers**: ...
- **lengths of time**: ...
- **sums of money**: ...
- **populations of towns and countries**: ...

Remember ...

GERMAN	ENGLISH
null, null, ...	double oh, ...
eins Komma zwei Kilometer	one point two kilometres
die **A** dreihundertachtzig	the **A** three, eight, oh
zweihundertzwanzig	two hundred and twenty
hundertfünfzehn	a/one hundred and fifteen
dreieinhalb	three and a half
115.100 (einhundertfünfzehn-tausend einhundert)	115,100 (one hundred and fifteen thousand one hundred)
£11,50 (elf Pfund fünfzig)	£11.50 (eleven pounds fifty)

Sieh dir zum Schluss an, welche Wörter man für den Wert 'null' in verschiedenen Situationen benutzt. Übertrage die Liste in dein Übungsheft.

You write – you say			You write – you say		
football	1 – 0	one nil	**telephone**	0146	oh, one, four, six
tennis	15 – 0	fifteen love	**smaller than 0**	0.8	nought point eight
temperature	0°C	zero degrees centigrade		0.804	nought point eight oh four

32 one/ones

You use *one* or *ones* when you don't want to repeat a noun which has been mentioned before.

die 'Ersatzwörter' *one/ones*

Lies die Sprechblasen und finde heraus, was sich die Leute ansehen.
Finde die englischen Entsprechungen für 'mir gefallen die schwarzen wirklich gut', 'wir haben bessere gesehen', 'dieses sieht groß genug aus', 'diese sind billiger', 'ein Trainingsanzug' und 'ich wünschte, ich könnte mir einen leisten'.

In der ersten Sprechblase sind drei *phrases* markiert. Finde weitere elf *phrases* mit *one/ones* in den Sprechblasen und markiere sie. (Die Lösung steht unten auf der Seite.)

In a sports shop

HINT

How to use *one/ones*:
- *adjective* }
- *the* } + *one/ones*
- *which* }
- *this, that* + *one*
- *these, those* + *ones*

You can use *one* instead of an indefinite article + noun:
afford a bag → *afford one*

Lege in deinem Übungsheft eine dreispaltige Tabelle an. Trage in die zweite Spalte die *phrases* mit *one/ones* ein. Ergänze dann die erste und dritte Spalte. Sieh dir die deutschen Entsprechungen an. Weshalb, denkst du, bereitet Lernenden die Verwendung von *one/ones* gelegentlich Probleme?

phrases with … nouns	one/ones	
1. the black **sweatshirts**	the black **ones**	*die schwarzen*
the black **sweatshirt**	the black **one**	*das schwarze*
a black **sweatshirt**	a black **one**	*ein schwarzes*
2. …	a stronger **one**	…
…	…	…
5. afford **a tennis racket**	…	…
…	…	…

Sieh dir den unvollständigen Merksatz und die Hinweise an. Ergänze den Merksatz und übertrage ihn mit dem Hinweis in dein Übungsheft.

Man verwendet ________/________, wenn man ein bereits erwähntes ______________ nicht wiederholen möchte: *One/ones* können nach einem ______________, nach *the* und nach ___________ verwendet werden. Nach *this/that* gebraucht man _______; nach *these/those* gebraucht man _______. Mit *one* kann man auch einen unbestimmten ______________ + Nomen ersetzen.

an exercise

Sieh dir diese Kurzdialoge an. Übertrage sie in dein Übungsheft und vervollständige sie sinnvoll mit *one/ones*. (Die Lösung steht unter den Sätzen.)

1. What's your favourite team?
   – I don't have …. I usually support the weaker ….
2. Did you see the match on TV?
   – Do you mean … that ended with a penalty shootout?
3. Shall we go to the outdoor or the indoor pool?
   – Let's go to … that's open.
4. Who is that swimmer?
   – Which …? … in the blue swimming trunks? That's Neal.

a stronger one, better ones; this one, that one, which one; these ones, those ones; the one I've got, the ones here; afford one, buy one // 1. one, one; 2. the one; 3. the one; 4. one, the one

Satzteile

Sieh dir die Tabelle und den Hinweis an.
Ordne dann die Lautschrift dem richtigen Wort zu und ergänze die deutschen Fachausdrücke:

Prädikat • Adverbial
Subjekt • Objekt

Übertrage die Tabelle und den Hinweis in dein Übungsheft.

33 parts of a sentence

1. four names

If you can identify parts of a sentence, you can often understand difficult sentences better.

ENGLISH		GERMAN
['ɒbdʒɪkt]	subject	___________
[əd'vɜ:biəl]	verb	___________
[vɜ:b]	object →	*Ob…*
['sʌbdʒɪkt]	adverbial	___________

HINT: The English word *verb* has two German meanings.
As a part of a sentence it is *Prädikat*. As a word class it is *Verb*.

Sieh dir das Bild und den Text an und finde heraus, wovon Dave träumte.

Finde die englischen Entsprechungen für 'er war versteckt hinter…', 'der Safe enthielt …', 'dann muss ich verschwinden' und 'ich habe eine der Alarmanlagen ausgeschaltet'.

Im Text sind drei Prädikate markiert, die aus einem Vollverb bzw. Hilfsverben und einem Vollverb bestehen.
Finde weitere dreizehn Prädikate und markiere sie. (Die Lösung steht unten auf der Seite.)

2. more about the verb

Dave 'Fingers' Powell **was dreaming**. In his dream he was standing in front of a small safe. It was hidden behind a Renoir painting. Dave had entered the large house easily. He **knew** the safe contained diamonds and cash. He looked at his watch. "I've got ten minutes," he told himself. "Then I must escape. I have switched off one alarm.I hope they haven't hidden another."

This **was going to be** his last job. He would never have to work again. For the rest of his life he would be able to lie on the beach.

HINT: As a part of a sentence the ***verb*** can consist of …
– a main verb only (*knew, contained, …*) or
– one or more auxiliary verbs plus a main verb (*was dreaming, was going to be …*).

Sieh dir den unvollständigen Merksatz und die Hinweise auf dieser Seite an. Vervollständige dann den Merksatz und übertrage ihn in dein Übungsheft.

Die englische Bezeichnung für den Satzteil *Prädikat* ist ______________. Das *verb* kann aus nur ______________ Vollverb bestehen (*knew, contained,* ________________ etc). Das *verb* kann auch aus einem oder ______________ Hilfsverben und einem ________________ bestehen (*was dreaming, was going to be,* ____________________).

was standing, was hidden, had entered, contained, looked, 've got, told, must escape, have found, hope, haven't hidden, would have to work, would be able to lie

3. more about the subject and object

Sieh dir die Fortsetzung des Traums an. Finde die englischen Entsprechungen für 'verschiedene Zahlenkombinationen', 'mehr Probleme als alle bisherigen', 'er durfte sie nicht vergeuden', 'ein plötzliches Geräusch erschreckte ihn' und 'wenn sie den Safe überprüfen würden, …'.

Dave's dream (part II)

'Fingers' put on **his gloves** and started to open **the safe**. **He** tried **different combinations of numbers**.

The first combination that he tried didn't open **it**. This safe was causing more problems than all the others.

The burglar looked at his watch. He had another seven minutes. He couldn't waste them.

A sudden noise startled him. Somebody had opened the front door of the house. The owners of the diamonds had entered the house. If they checked the safe, they would discover the crime.

	subject	object
noun/name:	'Fingers'	his gloves
	…	…
pronoun:	He	it
	…	…
expanded noun:	The first combination that he tried	different combinations of numbers
	…	…

Im Text sind je drei Subjekte und Objekte markiert. Markiere die restlichen Subjekte und Objekte. (Die Lösung steht unten.) Übertrage dann diese Tabelle in dein Übungsheft und ergänze je zwei Subjekte und Objekte aus dem Text für 'Nomen/Eigennamen', 'Pronomen' und 'erweiterte Nomen'.

HINT

subject pronouns	*object pronouns*
I	me
you	you
she, he, it	her, his, it
we	us
you	you
they	them

Das ____________ und ____________ eines Satzes können aus …

– einem Nomen oder ____________

– einem ____________________ oder

– einem erweiterten ____________ bestehen.

Außer für *you* und *it* werden für Subjekt und Objekt unterschiedliche ____________________ verwendet.

Sieh dir den Merksatz und die zwei Hinweise an. Ergänze den Merksatz und übertrage ihn mit den Hinweisen in dein Übungsheft.

HINT

The *subject* and *object* of a sentence can consist of …
– a noun or a name
– a pronoun
– an expanded noun.

4. more about adverbials

Hier erfährst du, wie der Traum endete. Achte auf die unterschiedlich markierten Adverbiale.

In less than five minutes 'Fingers' had found the right combination.

He opened the door **slowly and quietly**. **There, in the safe,** he could see them … He had **often** had difficult jobs, but he had **never** failed. **Tomorrow** he would be in the Caribbean. He stretched out his hands … and heard the alarm.

Dave woke up. He wasn't on a beach in the Caribbean. He was in his prison bed. The safe had had a secret alarm. That had been his last job for a long, long time.

HINT

As a part of a sentence, an adverbial can be
– an adverb (= one word)
or
– an expanded noun.

adverbial of manner	adverbial of frequency
slowly	often
…	…

adverbial of place	adverbial of time
there	in less than ten minutes
…	…

Lies den Hinweis und sieh dir die Tabellen an. Übertrage sie in dein Übungsheft und ergänze die restlichen *adverbials* aus dem Text.

subjects: this safe, the burglar, he, he, a sudden noise, somebody, the owners of the diamonds, they, they; objects: more problems than all the others, his watch, another seven minutes, them, him, the front door of the house, the house; the safe, the crime

Personalpronomen

Sieh dir diese Geschichte an und finde heraus, was Sue beim Babysitten passierte.

Finde dann die englischen Entsprechungen für 'meine Freundin ... erzählte sie mir', 'sie brachte sie ins Bett', 'sie baten sie, die Türen zu verschließen', 'du musst so lange wie möglich mit ihm sprechen', 'wir teilen dir mit, von wo er anruft', 'ihr müsst alle schnell das Haus verlassen' und 'bevor er euch alle angreift'.

Im Text sind vier Personalpronomen markiert. Finde und markiere weitere sechs Personalpronomen mit unterschiedlicher Bedeutung vor einem Verb und weitere sechs nach einem Verb oder einer Präposition.

Sieh dir diese unvollständige Tabelle und den Hinweis an.
Ergänze die Tabelle. (Die Lösung steht unten auf der Seite.)

Übertrage die Tabelle in dein Übungsheft.

Sieh dir den unvollständigen Merksatz und noch einmal den Hinweis an.
Ergänze den Merksatz und übertrage ihn zusammen mit dem Hinweis in dein Übungsheft.

34 personal pronouns

You use personal pronouns so that you don't have to repeat nouns or names.

Believe it, or not.

I heard this story last week. My friend Sue told **it** to **me**: **She** was babysitting in a large house. She had told the children a story and then she put them to bed. Now everything was quiet in the house.

Suddenly the phone rang. She picked it up. She heard a man; he was laughing and shouting hysterically. She couldn't understand him at all.

She put the phone down, but soon it rang again. She decided to call the police. They asked her to lock the doors and windows. "If it happens again, you must talk to him as long as possible," they said. "We will tell you where he is calling from. Phone us back if you are frightened."

Again the phone rang and she heard the man laughing and shouting. She tried talking to him, but he didn't listen to her. He put the phone down.

Then a police officer phoned back. "You must all get out of the house quickly. He's phoning from somewhere in the house. Get out before he attacks you all."

personal pronouns

	subject pronouns	object pronouns
	singular	
1st person	______	______
2nd person	you	you
3rd person	she	______
	______	______
	______	it
	plural	
1st person	______	______
2nd person	you	you
3rd person	______	______

Personal pronouns can go before a verb or after a verb or a preposition.

The personal pronouns before a verb are called subject pronouns.

The personal pronouns after a verb or a preposition are called object pronouns.

______________ können ______ einem Verb stehen (_____ *was laughing and shouting hysterically*). Diese Pronomen nennt man *subject* ____________.

Sie können auch ________ einem Verb oder einer ____________ stehen (*She put* ________ *to bed. You must talk to* ______ *as long as possible*).

Diese Personalpronomen nennt man ______________________.

subject pronouns: I, you, she, he, it, we, you, they
object pronouns: me, you, her, him, it, us, you, them

35 possessives: my, mine, …

1. possessive determiners

You use possessives to say that something ‘belongs’ to a person.

I've bought this postcard for **my** parents. Do you like it?

I've put **your** new ski suit in this wardrobe.

Tell Sandra I've found her purse.

Peter has left his anorak on the coach.

Look at the cat in its basket. Isn't it sweet?

I'm starving. Where are our cheese and tomato sandwiches?

Don't forget to collect your ski passes.

Someone has left their goggles on the table.

Why didn't Tim and David empty their rucksacks?

Ten and a cat in a room (part I)

personal pronouns	possessive determiners
I	my cap
you	… ski suit
she	…
he	…
it	…
we	…
you	…
they	…
someone	… goggles

Possessivbegleiter und Possessivpronomen

Sieh dir die Sätze links an und finde die englischen Entsprechungen für ‘Gefällt sie dir?’, ‘ich habe ihre Geldbörse gefunden’, ‘in ihrem Korb’, ‘ich bin am Verhungern’, ‘vergesst nicht eure Skipässe abzuholen’, ‘ihre Rucksäcke’ und ‘jemand hat seine Skibrille liegen lassen’.

In zwei Sätzen sind Possessivbegleiter markiert. Finde und markiere die Possessivbegleiter in den restlichen Sätzen. Lege in deinem Übungsheft eine Tabelle an – wie in dem Beispiel – und vervollständige sie.

Possessive determiners are used in front of a noun (*my* parents, *your* new ski suit).

After the pronouns *everyone, someone, anyone* and *no one* you usually use the possessive determiner *their* (*Someone* has left *their goggles* …).

HINT

Possessivbegleiter drücken aus, dass einer ________________ etwas ‘gehört’. Man verwendet sie ________ einem Nomen (*my parents*, ____________________, ________________________). Mit *everyone*, ______________, ______________ und ______________ benutzt man *their* als ______________________ (*someone* → *their goggles*, *everyone* → ______ *goggles*, *no one* → ____________).

Ergänze diesen unvollständigen Merksatz. Die beiden Hinweise helfen dir dabei. Übertrage dann den Merksatz in dein Übungsheft.

2. an exercise: a problem for you?

the boys' gloves – *Sally's* wallet – *Lisa's* ski pass – *Tom's and Janet's* sandwiches – *Simon's and my* money – *John's and your* CDs – *Luke's* keys – *the cat's* dinner – *the dog's* dinner – *Mr Dobb's and Miss Baker's* skis

the boys' gloves	their gloves	*ihre Handschuhe*
Sally's wallet	…	*ihre Brieftasche*
Lisa's ski pass	…	*ihr …*
…	…	…

Übertrage diese dreispaltige Liste in dein Übungsheft und vervollständige sie. (Die Lösung steht du unten.)

Sieh dir noch einmal deine Liste an. Weshalb, denkst du, haben Lernende Probleme mit *her* und *their* sowie mit *his* und *its*?

their …; her …; her …; their …; our …; your …; his …; its …; its …; their …

3. possessive pronouns

Sieh dir diese Sätze an und finde die englischen Entsprechungen für 'das ist meine', 'wenn dieser Skianzug deiner ist, ...', 'Warum trägt Peter nicht ...?', 'Handy', 'Internetzugang', 'lasst sie nicht ... liegen' und 'ihre sind beide rot'.

In zwei Sätzen sind Possessivpronomen markiert. Finde fünf weitere und markiere sie.

Ten and a cat in a room (part II)

Hey, give me that cap. It's mine.
If this ski suit is yours, where is Emma's?
Why isn't Peter wearing an anorak?
The driver has found his.
Laura's mobile phone is much better.
Hers has internet access.
Don't eat those sandwiches.
They're ours. We're starving!
Sam, Ben, these ski passes are yours.
Don't leave them on the bed.
Those rucksacks don't belong to Emma and Lisa. Theirs are both red.

Lege dir nun in deinem Übungsheft eine Tabelle an – wie in dem Beispiel – und ordne den Personalpronomen die Possessivbegleiter und die Possessivpronomen zu.

personal pronouns	possessive determiners	possessive pronouns
I	my	mine
you	your	…
she	…	…
he	…	…
it	…	xxx
we	…	…
you	…	…
they	…	…

You can use possessive pronouns when you don't want to repeat a noun that has already been mentioned. Possessive pronouns stand alone in a sentence. They can be the subject (*Hers has internet access*) or the object (*The driver has found his*). There is no possessive pronoun for *it*.

Sieh dir diese drei Sätze an und übertrage sie ins Deutsche. Weshalb, denkst du, haben Lernende Probleme mit diesen *determiners* und *pronouns*?

Where are my shoes?
(Wo sind ...?)
These here aren't mine.
(Das sind ....)

Is this your rucksack,
or is that yours?
(Ist das ...,
oder ist der ...?)

Sieh dir den Merksatz und den Hinweis oben an. Ergänze den Merksatz und übertrage ihn in dein Übungsheft.

______________________ werden benutzt, wenn man ein bereits erwähntes __________ nicht wiederholen möchte *(Is this Tom's cap? – No, it's mine)*. Sie stehen immer ____________. Possessivpronomen können ___________ (______ *has internet access)* oder ______________ *(The driver has found* ________) eines Satzes sein.

4. an exercise: possessive determiner or possessive pronoun?

Sieh dir diese Sätze an. Übertrage sie, ergänzt um die richtigen *possessives*, in dein Übungsheft.

1. Have you seen … boots? I think these are ….
   my/mine — you/yours
2. Can I borrow … socks? Sandy wanted to give me …, but she forgot.
   your/yours — her/hers
3. Ask Emma and Lisa if they've found … ski passes. Mr Dobbs has found ….
   their/theirs — your/yours
4. Those sandwiches are … Sam and Ben aren't hungry. You can have ….
   our/ours — their/theirs
5. Does … mobile phone work here? … doesn't.
   your/yours — My/Mine

1 my, yours; 2 your, hers; 3 their, yours; 4 ours, theirs; 5 your, mine

36 prepositions

Präpositionen

1. the easy bit

1
Where are my car keys?
I've looked **on the fridge.**
I've looked in the fridge.
They're not behind the microwave.
I've looked on top of the TV.
Are they under the table?
What's that in front of the stereo?

2
Can you take me **to the office?**
I'm late.
If you drive along Tower Street towards the traffic lights, it's only a short walk from there.
I'll go across the road and walk through the park.

3
We must leave **before 8 o'clock.**
I was late on Friday.
You can phone me during my lunchhour or after 4 o'clock.
I'll be there till 6 o'clock.
I should be home at about 7.

Last minute rush

Sieh dir die Sprechblasen an und finde heraus, weshalb dieser Mann so nervös ist.

Finde die englischen Entsprechungen für 'allerhöchste Eile', 'Was ist das dort vor der Stereoanlage?', 'ich bin spät dran', 'ich überquere die Straße', 'ich bin am Freitag zu spät gekommen' und 'ich bin bis sechs Uhr dort'.

Some prepositions consist of more than one word: *in front of, instead of, etc.*

Many prepositions belong to three groups:

prepositions of direction: ☐
Can you take me to the office?
…
prepositions of time: ☐
…
prepositions of place: ☐
…

In den Sprechblasen sind drei *phrases* markiert. Finde weitere *phrases* mit Präpositionen der Richtung, der Zeit und des Ortes in den Sprechblasen und markiere sie.

Trage in diese Tabelle die jeweils richtige Nummer der Sprechblase ein. (Die Lösung steht unten.) Übertrage die Tabelle mit je zwei Beispielsätzen in dein Übungsheft.

2. the tricky bit

I'm still waiting for **an answer to** my questions.
Emma was so **proud of** her work.
What does that mean **in German?**
Why are your keys lying **on the floor?**
It's **two weeks to** Xmas and I haven't bought any presents.
Must we **drive to** London tomorrow?
Your suggestion should be **acceptable to** everybody.
Give the present to him now.

Sieh dir diese Sätze an. Finde die englischen Entsprechungen für 'eine Antwort auf …', 'stolz auf', 'zwei Wochen bis Weihnachten' und 'nach London fahren'. Lies dann den Hinweis links unten. Weshalb, denkst du, haben Lernende häufig Probleme mit Präpositionen?

Prepositions can be difficult because …

English	your language
one preposition	several prepositions
several prepositions	one preposition
a preposition	no preposition
one place in a sentence	another place in a sentence

3. even trickier?

What did you **talk** to him **about?**

He was boring. He didn't want to tell me where he**'s from** or what he**'s interested in.**

Well, he was better-looking than the guy that you **danced with** at the disco last Saturday.

Sieh dir den Dialog an. Übertrage zwei der Sätze mit ihrer deutschen Entsprechung in dein Übungsheft. Vergleiche die Stellung der Präpositionen und markiere die Präpositionen.

The best advice is: Learn prepositions together with their nouns, verbs and adjectives.

direction: 2; time: 3; place: 1

unbestimmte Mengenangaben

Lies den Text und finde heraus, welche Dinge Victor verkauft.
Schlage nach, wo sich die Länder befinden.

Finde die englischen Entsprechungen für '(er) hat einen Stand auf dem Markt', 'neuen Schmuck', 'einige Ringe', 'er verkauft wahrscheinlich alle Ringe', 'die meisten Halsketten', 'die Leute interessieren sich nicht für sie' und 'er hat noch keine von den großen Figuren verkauft'.

37 quantifiers

You use quantifiers to say
– how many things or
– how much of something you are talking about.

1. quantifiers with *countable nouns*

Victor Dhlamini has a stall at the market. He sells a lot of clothes from Africa. Sometimes he sells over 100 T-shirts in one day. His stall always has many different things.

This week he has new jewellery and leather goods. He has some rings and necklaces from Zimbabwe. He will probably sell all the rings and most of the necklaces.

He has some leather bags and some leather shoes from Tanzania. He hasn't sold many bags and he has sold no shoes. He doesn't know why people aren't interested in them.

Victor has twenty wooden figures from Mozambique. He hasn't sold any large figures – they are probably too expensive. He has sold a few smaller figures, about five so far.

Victor Dhlamini's stall at Totnes market

Sieh dir nun diese Tabelle mit einem unvollständigen Text an.
Finde die fehlenden Mengenangaben im Text oben und trage sie ein.
(Die Lösung steht unten auf der Seite.)

Ordne den vier unbeschrifteten Kreisen Mengenangaben zu.

Übertrage die Tabelle mit der Prozentskala und dem Hinweis unten in dein Übungsheft.
Füge die deutschen Entsprechungen für die Mengenangaben hinzu.

Hopefully I'll sell *all the* rings.

I'll probably sell *most of the* necklaces.

I sell __________ clothes from Africa.

My stall has ________ different things.

This week I have ________ rings and necklaces.

I also have ________ leather bags and ________ leather shoes.

I'm quite happy; I've sold ________ small figures.

Unfortunately, I have ________ sold ________ bags.

I've sold ________ shoes at all.

I have_____ sold ________ large figures.

All these quantifiers are used with plural forms of nouns.

HINT

2. an exercise

Ordne die Sätze einander zu, die sinnvoll zusammen passen.
(Die Lösung steht unter den Sätzen.)

Last Wednesday ...	**So, at the end of the day ...**
1. Victor sold a lot of T-shirts. →	a. he didn't have any on his stall.
2. he didn't sell all the necklaces.	b. he had as many as in the morning.
3. he could only sell a few rings.	c. he only had a few left.
4. he didn't sell any bags.	d. some were still there.
5. he sold all the shoes.	e. he had to take most of them home.

1 c, 2 d, 3 e, 4 b, 5 a

a lot of, many, some, some, some, a few, not ... many, no, not ... any //

3. quantifiers for countable and uncountable nouns: a problem for you?

In diesen Sprechblasen sind sechs Mengenangaben unterschiedlich markiert. Übertrage sie ins Deutsche.

Weshalb, denkst du, bereiten einige Mengenangaben Lernenden Probleme, wenn sie ihre Gedanken ins Englische übertragen?

					countable nouns	uncountable nouns
You can use	most quantifiers			with	✔	✔
You must use	________	and	________	with	✔	
You must use	________	and	________	with		✔

Sieh dir diese unvollständige Tabelle an. Finde in den Sprechblasen die beiden *quantifiers*, die nur mit *countable* und die beiden, die nur mit *uncountable nouns* verwendet werden. Ergänze die Tabelle und übertrage sie in dein Übungsheft.

4. quantifiers in questions

1. Victor, have you sold ____________ those beautiful bags?
2. Do ____________ customers try to get a better price?
3. Do you have ____________ older customers, Victor?
4. Are there ____________ stalls that sell things from India?
5. Why do you only sell ____________ wooden figures?
6. When are you going to get ____________ new jewellery?
7. How ____________ profit a week do you make?
8. How ____________ customers do you have on a good day?

a few – all – a lot of – any – many – most – much – some

Hier hast du acht unvollständige Fragen und Mengenangaben. Vervollständige jede Frage mit einer Mengenangabe. Die Kreise geben einen Hinweis darauf, was in jede Lücke gehört. (Die Lösung steht unten auf der Seite.)

5. some useful expressions to talk about quantities

Useful expressions

almost all my customers
fast alle meine Kunden
not all my customers
nicht alle meine Kunden
(almost) all my life
(fast) mein ganzes Leben

most people
die meisten Leute
most of the time
die meiste Zeit

(not) such a lot of luck
(nicht) so viel Glück

(not) so many people
(nicht) so viele Leute
(far) too many people
(viel) zu viele Leute

(far) too much news
(viel) zu viele Nachrichten
How much is it?
Wie viel kostet das?
I haven't got **much time**.
Ich habe nicht viel Zeit.

in **a few** days
in einigen/ein paar Tagen

in **the last few** years
in den letzten Jahren

a little more
etwas mehr

Any colour will do.
Die Farbe spielt keine Rolle.

I have **hardly any** luck
Ich habe kaum Glück.

Sieh dir diese *phrases* mit Mengenangaben an und übertrage sie mit ihrer deutschen Entsprechung in dein Übungsheft.

1. all; 2. most; 3. a lot of; 4. any; 5. a few; 6. some; 7. much; 8. many

38 questions

Fragen

Sieh dir das Bild und die Sprechblasen an.
Finde heraus, weshalb Patrick Ealing festgenommen wurde.

Finde die englischen Entsprechungen für ‘Haben Sie das Geld am Freitag Nachmittag auf ein Konto in der Schweiz überwiesen?’, ‘Haben Sie mit Kelly seit Montag gesprochen?’, ‘Sagen Sie die Wahrheit?’, ‘Reist sie oft ins Ausland?’ und ‘Wird Kelly an Sie denken?’

In den Sprechblasen sind Subjekte und Formen des *simple past, present perfect, present progressive, simple present* sowie Futur- und Modalformen markiert.
Lies den Hinweis oben rechts und markiere dann die restlichen Fragen auf gleiche Weise.

It is easy to make questions:
You put an auxiliary verb before the subject.
After the subject you have
a form of the main verb.

1. finding the forms

On Moday detectives arrested Patrick Ealing.
They are still looking for his girlfriend, Kelly Brown.

Five million pounds missing from a London bank

1 **Did you break into** City Finance’s computer system last week?
Did you send the money to a bank account in Switzerland on Friday afternoon?
Did Kelly take the money out of Bankhaus Kleinmann on Monday morning? Tell us the truth, Patrick.

2 **Do you have** a house in Switzerland?
Does Kelly speak French?
Does she often travel abroad?

3 **Are you telling** the truth, Patrick?
Is Kelly hiding in Switzerland now? Is she using a false passport or a different name?

4 **Are you going to talk to** us, Patrick?
And think about this:
Is Kelly going to wait ten years till you come out of prison?

7 She’s a rich woman now Patrick.
Will Kelly think of you when you’re in prison?
Will she take the money?
When will she marry another man?

6 **Can you help** us, Patrick?
Should we leave you alone for a few minutes?

5 **Have you spoken to** Kelly since Monday?
Has she told you where she is?

Write the numbers of the speech bubbles in the boxes.

Sieh dir nun die Sprechblasen und diese sechs Aussagen über verschiedene Zeiten an. Ordne die Sprechblasen den Aussagen zu. In einigen Fällen helfen die *adverbs* und *adverbials of time* in den Fragen.
(Die Lösung steht unten auf der Seite.)

2. organizing the forms: a checklist about different times

the past	from the past to the present	the present (*now, at the moment*)	the future
☐	☐	☐	☐ and ☐

with modals ☐

about permanent situations, regular events and actions (*often, regularly, every …*) ☐

about the past: 1; the time from the past to the present: 5; the present: 3; the future: 4 and 7; for a permanent situation, regular events and actions: 2; with modals: 6

to talk about the past:

Did you ______________ *City Finance's computer system* __________________?

to talk about the time from _______________ to ____________________:

Have you ____?

to talk about the ________________:

Are you ____?

to talk about __________________ with "will":

Will ____?

to talk about the __________________ with "going to":

Is Kelly ____?

to talk about _________________________, regular events, ____________:

Do you ____?

with modals:

____?

Sieh dir diese unvollständige Tabelle, die Sprechblasen und die Checkliste auf Seite 66 an und vervollständige die Tabelle.

Übertrage die Tabelle dann in dein Übungsheft und füge je einen weiteren Beispielsatz aus den Sprechblasen hinzu.

3. how to make questions

- Für ____________________ über **die Vergangenheit** braucht man nur __________ Form: *did* + *subject* + _______________________.
- Für die Zeit **von der** ____________________ **bis zur Gegenwart** gibt es _______ Formen: *have* **oder** _________ + *subject* + *past* ____________________.
  Für *he, she, it* verwendet man _________ (________ *she told you where she is?*).
- Um über **die Gegenwart** zu fragen, braucht man eine ___________ von *be* + ________________ + *present participle* (___________ *you telling the truth?* _______ *she* ________________ *a false passport?*).
- Für **die** _____________ verwendet man *will* + __________ + ______________ (________ *she* ____________ *the money?*) **oder** eine Form von ______ + *subject* + *going to* + ________________ (________ *you going* ________________ *us?* ________ *Kelly* _________________________ *ten years?*).
- Für **Dauerzustände** und für **Dinge, die** ____________________ geschehen, braucht man ________ oder *does* + *subject* + ____________________.
  Für *he, she, it* verwendet man ________ (_______ *Kelly* ____________ *French?*).
- Nach **Modalverben** verwendet man einen __________________ (*Can you* ____________ *us?* ____________ *we* ____________ *you alone for a few minutes?*).

Sieh dir nun diesen unvollständigen Merksatz und den Hinweis sowie die Sprechblasen an.

HINT

- infinitives: *talk, hide, tell*
- present participles: *talking, hiding, telling*
- past participles: *talked, hidden, told*
- forms of *be*: *am, are, is*

Vervollständige den Merksatz und übertrage ihn zusammen mit dem Hinweis in dein Übungsheft.

- For questions with *be* as a main verb, look at pages 20–23.
- For questions with *do* as a main verb, look at pages 28–29.
- For questions with *have* as a main verb, look at pages 30–31.
- For more information also look at the entries for *can, have to, may, modals* and *must*.

Sieh dir diese Entscheidungsfragen und Antworten aus Patricks Verhör an und finde die englischen Entsprechungen für 'warum sollte ich ...?', 'ich habe mit ihr am ... zum letzten Mal gesprochen', 'ich schwöre, dass ich es nicht war' und 'in der Nähe von'.

Ordne die Fragen und Antworten einander zu und markiere die Kurzantworten wie in dem Beispiel. (Die Lösung steht unten auf der Seite.)

3. *yes/no*-questions and short answers

1. **Did you break** into that computer system last week?
2. **Do you and Kelly have** a house in Switzerland?
3. **Are you telling** the truth?
4. **Have you spoken** to Kelly since Monday?
5. **Will Kelly think** of you when you're in prison?
6. **Will she take** the money and marry another man?

a. Of course she will. But why should I go to prison?
b. No, I haven't. I last spoke to her on Friday before she left.
c. No, she won't. She hasn't taken any money.
d. Yes, I am. Why should I lie?
e. **No, I didn't.** I swear it wasn't me.
f. Yes, we do. It's near Bern.

Hier hast du drei Fragen. Vervollständige nun die drei Kurzantworten. Hilfe findest du in dem Hinweis rechts. (Die Lösung steht unten auf der Seite.)

Übertrage den Hinweis und die Sprechblasen in dein Übungsheft.

HINT
- In answers to *yes/no*-questions you repeat the auxiliary from the question.
- In a positive answer, you use a positive form.
- In a negative answer, you use a negative form.
- If you only say *yes* or *no*, your answer may sound impolite.

Vergleiche die englischen und deutschen Antworten zu diesen Fragen. Weshalb können Lernende hier Probleme haben? (Achte auf den letzten Punkt des Hinweises oben.)

4. short answers – a problem for you ?

Did you send the money to Switzerland?	No, I didn't. Why are you asking me? *Nein. Warum fragen Sie mich?*
Does Kelly speak French?	Of course she does. We are often in France. *Natürlich. Wir sind oft in Frankreich.*

Sieh dir die Tabelle und die drei Begriffe rechts an. Ergänze die fehlenden Überschriften mit diesen Begriffen.

Vergleiche die Satzbaupläne der ersten vier Fragen: Wie unterscheidet sich Frage 1 von den Fragen 2 bis 4? Vergleiche auch die Stellung der Präposition im Englischen und Deutschen in Frage 3.

Übertrage die Tabelle und diesen Hinweis zu den Satzbauplänen in dein Übungsheft.

5. questions with question words

subject • auxiliary • form of the main verb

	question word	________	________	________	*object / adverbial*	
1.		*Did*	Kelly	*take*	the money?	
2.	**When**	*did*	she	*take*	it?	(Wann ...?)
3.	**Who**	*did*	Kelly	*send*	the money **to?**	(An wen ...?)
4.	**What**	*did*	you	*do*	in the bank?	(Was ...?)
5.			**Who**	*sent*	it to Bern?	(Wer ...?)
6.			**What**	*happened*	last Friday?	(Was ...?)

HINT
The word order in *yes/no*-questions and in questions with a question word is really the same.
When the question word is the subject of a sentence, you don't need *did*, *do* or *does* after the question word.

1e; 2f; 3d; 4b; 5a; 6c
Of course they did. / Yes, we will. / No, she hasn't.

39 question tags

Question tags are short questions at the end of positive or negative statements.
You often use a question tag when you want somebody to agree with you.

a. I'm sure he will.
b. No, we should leave Zurich tonight.
c. Yes, they have. He wasn't careful enough.
d. I'm afraid you can do nothing for him.
e. That's right. They're looking everywhere.
f. There's no way they'll find us in Brazil.

1. The police **have arrested** Patrick, **haven't** they?
2. They're looking for me now, aren't they?
3. Inspector Cluzot will try and find me, won't he?
4. We **shouldn't stay** in Switzerland, **should** we?
5. They won't find us in South America, will they?
6. I can't help Patrick, can I?

A new friend for Kelly

Frageanhängsel: ..., *nicht wahr?*

Sieh dir die sechs Fragen an. Finde heraus, was Kelly befürchtet und was sie vorhat. Lies dann die Antworten und ordne sie den Fragen zu. (Die Lösung steht unten.)

Finde die englischen Entsprechungen für 'die Polizei hat ... festgenommen', 'sie suchen mich jetzt', '(er) wird versuchen, mich zu finden', 'vorsichtig genug', 'leider kannst du nichts für ihn tun' und 'keinesfalls'.

Sieh dir die markierten Teile in den Fragen an. Markiere dann das Hilfsverb in den restlichen vier *question tags* und das Prädikat in den vorangehenden Aussagesätzen. (Die Lösung findest du unten.)

statement	question tag (with auxiliary)		reply
I **can't help** Patrick,	can I?	–	You can do nothing for him.
They **arrested** him on Monday,	**didn't** they?	–	Unfortunately they did.
The inspector **thinks** we're in Switzerland,	**doesn't** he?	–	I'm sure he does.
They **don't know** where we are,	**do** they?	–	No, but we must be careful.

Sieh dir nun diese Tabelle an und achte auf die markierten Teile. Lies dann den Hinweis unten links und sieh dir den unvollständigen Merksatz an.

HINT

- If there is an auxiliary in the statement, you use the same auxiliary for the question tag.
- For simple present and simple past you use a form of *do* for the tag: simple pres.: *do/don't* or *does/doesn't* simple past: *did/didn't*.
- A positive statement is usually followed by a negative question tag.
- A negative statement is usually followed by a positive question tag.

Wenn im Aussagesatz ein Hilfsverb verwendet wird, benutzt man das gleiche ________________ im *question tag*. In Sätzen im *simple present* und im ________________ benötigt man eine Form von __________ im *question tag*. Auf einen bejahten ______________________ folgt normalerweise ein ________________ *question tag*. Auf einen _____________ Aussagesatz folgt gewöhnlich ein *positive* ______________________.

Vervollständige nun den Merksatz. Übertrage ihn mit der Tabelle oben in dein Übungsheft.

have - haven't; 're - aren't; will - won't; shouldn't - should; won't - will; can't - can
1c, 2e, 3a, 4b, 5f, 6d

40 reflexive pronouns

Reflexivpronomen

Sieh dir an, was Rachel über ihren Skiurlaub sagt.

Finde die englischen Entsprechungen für 'wir haben uns wirklich gut amüsiert', '(Ski-)Lehrer', '(sie) hat sich am Knie verletzt' und 'er sagte er habe sich ... selbst beigebracht'.

Finde die Sätze mit *be proud of, injure* und *teach* und markiere Subjekte, Prädikate und Objekte wie im ersten Absatz.

1. reflexive pronouns as objects

You use reflexive pronouns when the subject and object of a sentence are the same person.

Ann, Dan, Andy and I **have enjoyed** our skiing trip. I think Ann and Dan **enjoyed** themselves although Ann had a stupid accident. Andy and I had a cool instructor. We really **enjoyed** ourselves with him.

The instructor said he was proud of me. I am proud of myself, too. I learned snowboarding this year.

Ann has injured her knee. She injured herself on the second day. The piste was icy and she lost control.

I was amazed how well Andy spoke German. He said he taught himself with an internet online course!!! I don't quite believe him. Does something like this really exist? ...

HINT
the same person:
I cooked a meal for myself.
different persons:
I cooked a meal for her.

Sieh dir diese vier Sätze, den Hinweis und die Tabelle an. Übertrage die Sätze mit ihren deutschen Entsprechungen und der vervollständigten Tabelle in dein Übungsheft. Weshalb, denkst du, können Lernende hier Probleme haben?

The instructor taught me snowboarding.
Der Skilehrer hat mir ...
I taught myself a lot of cool tricks.
Ich habe ...
On Saturday Dan said, "I'll make breakfast for you."
..., "Ich mache ..."
On Sunday he said, "Today you can make breakfast for yourselves."
..., "Heute könnt ihr ..."

personal pronouns		reflexive pronouns
...	me	...
you	you	yourself
...	her	...
...	him	...
it	it	itself
...	us	...
...	you	...
they	them	...

2. some verbs can be reflexive and some can't – a problem for you?

Übertrage diese Verben mit ihrer deutschen Entsprechung in dein Übungsheft. Schlage die Verben nach, die du nicht kennst. Weshalb haben Lernende mit Verben aus dem rechten Kasten häufig Probleme?

These verbs can be reflexive:

amuse oneself ✶ blame oneself ✶ cut oneself ✶ dry oneself ✶ enjoy oneself help oneself ✶ hurt oneself introduce oneself ✶ prepare oneself teach oneself

→ She blamed herself.
He blamed the other skier.

These aren't reflexive:

change ✶ complain ✶ concentrate decide ✶ feel ✶ hurry ✶ imagine meet ✶ move ✶ refer to ✶ relax show ✶ wonder ✶ worry

→ He has changed since we last met.
He worries less than before.

3. reflexive pronouns for emphasis

Finde in diesen Sprechblasen die englischen Entsprechungen für 'ich habe ... ganz alleine repariert', 'die Piste selbst ist fantastisch' und 'viel zu viele'.

Lies den Hinweis und finde dann die zwei Sätze, in denen das Reflexivpronomen nicht zur Betonung verwendet wird. – Die Lösung steht unten.

HINT
You can use reflexive pronouns to ...
- emphasize a noun or pronoun:
  → ***The hotel itself** was great.*
  → *I spoke to **the manager himself.***
- say that somebody did something without help:
  → *She **learned it herself.***
  (Nodody helped her.)

I can't dry myself ... / These rooms won't clean themselves.

41 relative clauses

Relative clauses give more information about people or things.

Relativsätze

1. defining relative clauses

Hotpotato is an internet company **which offers information and sells products to young people.**

One of their friends developed a website **that now gets more than 10,000 hits per day.**

However, when Suzi and Joan started their business, the banker who studied their plans didn't want to give them any money.

"There's a big difference," Suzi replied. "We offer something that will be popular with people for a long time."

The idea for the company came from two women **who met through the internet:** Suzi Wong and Jane Li.

Almost everybody who visits their site is really impressed.

"Aren't there too many people that are doing exactly the same thing?" he asked.

And Jane thought: Will he give us the money which will allow us to start a successful business?

Sieh dir die Informationen über *Hotpotato* an und finde heraus, welches Problem die Firmengründer hatten. Finde die englischen Entsprechungen für 'eine Internet-Firma, die Informationen anbietet', 'zwei Frauen, die sich über das Internet kennen lernten', 'eine Website, die jetzt mehr als ... angeklickt wird', 'fast jeder, der ... besucht', 'wir bieten etwas an, das ...' und 'das Geld, das es uns erlauben wird, ...'.

Im Text sind drei Relativsätze markiert. Finde weitere fünf und markiere sie.

relative pronouns

... who ...	... that ...	... which ...
two women who ...	______________	*an internet company which ...*
______________	______________	______________
______________	______________	

Sieh dir nun diese Tabelle an. Finde in den Sätzen die Nomen bzw. Pronomen, die vor den Relativpronomen *who, that* und *which* stehen, und ergänze die Tabelle.

① After ______________

you use ________ or ________.

② After ______________

you use ________ or ________.

things
people
who – that – which

Ergänze nun die Sätze in der Sprechblase mit den Wörtern aus der Wolke. (Die Lösung steht unten.) Übertrage beide Sätze zusammen mit der Tabelle in dein Übungsheft.

2. a note about word order in relative clauses

relative pronoun — verb

Suzie knows some products **which might sell** well on the internet.
Suzie kennt einige Produkte, **die sich** im Internet gut **verkaufen könnten.**

Jane has a friend **who will improve** their website.
Jane hat eine Freundin, **die** ihre Website **verbessern wird.**

In English there is no comma before a defining relative clause.

Vergleiche die englischen und deutschen Satzbaupläne. Finde zwei Unterschiede, die Lernenden häufig Probleme bereiten. – Einen davon kannst du nur in geschriebenen Texten erkennen.

3. an exercise: What is right – who or *which*?

1. The website has a splash screen ... attracts people's attention.
2. Younger surfers like the free stuff ... can be downloaded from the site.
3. Surfers ... like a good chat visit the site daily.
4. The e-mails ... reach the company often give positive feedback.
5. Everybody ... visits the site bookmarks it for their next visit.

Übertrage die fünf Sätze in dein Übungsheft und ergänze dabei das Relativpronomen. (Die Lösung findest du unten.)

.. = people: who, that ≠ = things: which, that // who: 3, 5; which: 1, 2, 4

Lies den Brief des Bankdirektors und einen Teil von Beckys E-Mail.

Finde die englischen Entsprechungen für '(er) sieht viel versprechend aus', 'beliebt', 'sie ist verantwortlich für', 'sie werden sich gut verkaufen', 'eine Geschäftsidee unterstützen'. Finde zwei Entsprechungen für 'die Produkte, die Sie verkaufen möchten'.

Vergleiche dann die beiden markierten Textstellen. Finde zwei weitere Stellen in den Briefen, die sich auf ähnliche Weise entsprechen, und markiere sie.

4. contact clauses

A contact clause is a relative clause without a relative pronoun. Contact clauses are often used in spoken and informal written English.

Dear Ms Wong

Thank you for your letter. **The business plan which you sent us** looks very promising. I'm sure the products that you want to sell will be very popular.

The person who you should see now is Becky Kamp. She is responsible for our business customers. She will phone you today. Another person that you should talk to is Mark Miller. He is our internet expert.

Yours sincerely,
Adam Brown, bank manager

Starting a business

"I really like **the business plan you sent us**. I also like the products you want to sell. I'm sure they will sell well. I'll be happy to support your business plan. The person you should talk to now is Mark. As you know, he is our internet expert."

Sieh dir diese Tabelle an: Wie unterscheiden sich die ersten beiden Relativsätze vom dritten und vierten? Wie unterscheiden sich der dritte und vierte Relativsatz vom fünften und sechsten?

main clause	relative clause		
		subject	
We offer something		that	will be popular with people.
We have found somebody		who	will help us.
We offer something	that	people	will like.
We have found somebody	who	we	can trust.
We offer something		people	will like.
We have found somebody		we	can trust.

Lies nun den unvollständigen Merksatz zusammen mit den Hinweisen rechts und oben sowie die Tabelle. Vervollständige den Merksatz. Übertrage die Tabelle mit dem Merksatz in dein Übungsheft.

Relativpronomen, die nicht ________________

des Relativsatzes sind, darf man weglassen.

Relativsätze ohne ______________________

heißen _______________ *clauses*.

If the relative pronoun isn't the subject of the relative clause, you can leave it out.

5. a puzzle: [hu:z] – *whose, who's (who is/who has)?*

Hier ist eine etwas seltsame Annonce. Lies den Hinweis rechts und finde heraus, für welche Wörter [hu:z] in den fünf Sätzen steht. (Die Lösung steht unten.)

Was sind die deutschen Entsprechungen für *whose*?

We need a second web-designer –
male or female ...

... [hu:z] young and dynamic.
... [hu:z] worked for a small company before.
... [hu:z] websites are popular with young people.
... [hu:z] work we can see on the web.

[hu:z] profile fits what we need?
If it's yours, contact ***Suzi@hot***

Whose can be a relative pronoun or a question word. It is used to talk about things that 'belong' to a person or a thing.

1. who's (= who is); 2. who's (= who has); 3. whose; 4. whose; 5. whose

42 ...s, ...'s, ...s'

Rail chaos

In 1995 Britain's railway system was privatized. The network was broken up and sold to private companies.

Passengers' opinions were divided. Some people thought competition would bring better train services.

However, a British Rail manager warned the government: "It's a big mistake. It's been done too quickly. Nobody knows whether the new system will work."

Lies diesen kurzen Text und finde heraus, weshalb die Bahnprivatisierung in Großbritannien problematisch war.

Finde dann die englischen Entsprechungen für 'das Streckennetz wurde aufgeteilt', 'die Meinungen der Reisenden gingen auseinander', 'Wettbewerb', und 'es wurde zu schnell durchgeführt'.

Sieh dir nun den Hinweis und die sechs Kästen darunter an.

...s is used for
- the plural of most nouns (*an accident, several accidents*)
- the simple present, 3rd person singular of full verbs (*Nobody wants ...*)

...'s is used after pronouns and nouns
- for the short form of *is* (*It's not clear ... / The Transport Minister's trying to help.*)
- for the short form of *has* (*He's tried to help. The Prime Minister's agreed to do it.*)

...'s is also used at the end of nouns to show that something 'belongs' to one person (*a reporter's comments*)

...s' is used at the end of nouns to show that something 'belongs' to more than one person (*some reporters' opinions*)

1. **plural form: *s*** ____________
2. **simple present 3rd person singular: *s*** ____________
3. **short form of *is*: *'s*** ____________
4. **short form of *has*: *'s*** ____________
5. **possessive, singular: *'s*** ____________
6. **possessive, plural: *s'*** ____________

Finde im Text oben je ein Beispiel für jeden Kasten und trage es ein. (Die Lösung steht unten auf der Seite.)

an exercise

Four years later, after a series of **accidents**, **Britain's** railways were in crisis. ☐ ☐

Then, in 2000 and 2001, **passengers** died in two very serious accidents. ☐

Suddenly, **passengers'** opinions were in all the newspapers and on television. ☐

Many asked, "**Who's** responsible for safety?" ☐

Others said, "Anyone **who's** travelled by train **knows** the system is bad." ☐ ☐

"**It's** time we had a system **that's** safe and efficient." ☐ ☐

"During the past three years **it's** gone from bad to worse." ☐

"The rail **companies** should be punished. The **companies'** bosses should be sent to jail." ☐ ☐

"Nobody **feels** responsible. Not one person **thinks** of the **passengers'** safety. All that **counts** is profit." ☐ ☐ ☐ ☐

Sieh dir die sechs Kästen oben und diesen Text an. Entscheide dann, wofür ***...s, ...'s*** oder ***...s'*** in den blauen Wörtern jeweils steht und trage die entsprechende Nummer ein. (Die Lösung steht unten auf der Seite.)

There's one more use of *'s*:
Let's talk about it later.
Let's do it now.
After *let*, the *'s* stands for *us*.

1. private companies; 2. nobody knows; 3. It's a ...; 4. It's been; 5. Britain's railway system; 6. passengers' opinions // 1, 5; 1; 6; 3; 4, 2; 3, 3; 4; 1, 6; 2, 2; 6, 2

Satzarten

Sieh dir die Tabelle an. Knobele die fehlenden Wörter für die deutschen Entsprechungen der vier Satzarten heraus und trage sie ein. (Die Lösung steht unten auf der Seite.)

43 sentence types

There are four sentence types: statement, question, command and exclamation.

1. the names of sentence types

positive **statement**	*bejahter* ________________
negative **statement**	________________ *Aussagesatz*
wh-**question**[1]	*Ergänzungs*________________
yes/no **question**[2]	*Entscheidungs*________________
positive **command**	________________ *Aufforderungssatz*
negative **command**	*verneinter* ________________
exclamation	*Ausrufesatz*

[1] also: question with question word
[2] also: question without question word

If 'positive' is …, then 'positive **command**' must be …. 'Negative' is …., so 'negative **statement**' is ….

2. examples of sentence types

Hier hast du sieben Beispiele für die vier Satzarten. Finde die englischen Entsprechungen für 'nicht sehr weit von', 'denke daran herauszufinden, wo …', 'SportlerInnen aus der ganzen Welt', 'bist du sicher, dass …?' und 'Vergiss nicht, … mitzubringen'.

Sieh dir nun die Sätze und die unvollständige Tabelle unten an. Trage die Nummer des jeweils passenden Satzes in die Tabelle ein. Übertrage die Tabelle in dein Übungsheft und vervollständige sie mit den Beispielsätzen. Die ersten Buchstaben der Sätze ergeben das Lösungswort für den Satz unter der Tabelle. (Die Lösung findest du unten.)

Olympic Games (I)

1. So much to remember!
2. Where were the first modern Olympic Games?
3. Olympia, the place of the first Olympic Games, isn't very far from Athens.
4. Remember to find out where the next Olympic Games are.
5. Today the Olympic Games are for athletes from all over the world.
6. Are you sure that they were in Athens in 1896?
7. Don't forget to bring the book about the 1960 Games in Rome.

positive statement	5	Today the Olympic Games …
negative statement	3	Olympia, …
wh-question	___	…
yes/no question	___	…
positive command	___	…
negative command	___	…
exclamation		…

The marathon runners were coming ________________ the entrance of the stadium.

HINT

Statements end with a full stop.
Questions end with a question mark.
Exclamations and commands can end with a full stop or an exclamation mark.

bejahter Aussagesatz, verneinter Aussagesatz, Ergänzungsfrage, Entscheidungsfrage, bejahter Aufforderungssatz, verneinter Aufforderungssatz // … are coming towards the entrance …

3. simple sentences and complex sentences

Olympic Games (II)

1 **Ancient Greece had a long tradition of athletic contests.** The Olympic Games were only one of these contests.

2 It is not clear **when the first games took place at Olympia.** But we know that such games took place more than 3,000 years ago.

3 The first documents that exist of the games at Olympia near Athens are from AD 776. Even after Greece was conquered by the Romans about 200 BC, the games took place every four years.

4 In AD 393 the Roman Emperor Theodosius abolished the Olympic Games because he thought that they were 'unchristian'. It took about 1,500 years before the first modern Olympic Games took place.

Hier hast du vier kurze Texte über die Olympischen Spiele. Finde heraus, weshalb sie einst verboten wurden.

Finde dann die englischen Entsprechungen für 'Sportwettkämpfe', 'solche Spiele fanden vor mehr als ... statt', 'aus dem Jahr 776 nach Christus', 'selbst nachdem Griechenland von ... erobert wurde', 'ungefähr 200 vor Christus', '(er) schaffte die Olympischen Spiele ab' und 'es dauerte ungefähr 1500 Jahre, bis ...'.

simple sentence (= main clause)

subject	verb	other parts
Ancient Greece	had	a long tradition of athletic contests.

complex sentence (= main clause + sub-clause)

subject	verb	other parts	conjunction	subject	verb	other parts
It	is not	clear	when	the first games	took place	at Olympia.

Sieh dir diese Beispiele für einen einfachen Satz (Hauptsatz) und für ein Satzgefüge (Hauptsatz + Nebensatz) an und lies dazu den Hinweis darunter.

In den Texten oben sind ein einfacher Satz und ein Nebensatz markiert. Finde einen weiteren einfachen Satz sowie sechs weitere Nebensätze und markiere sie. (Die Lösung steht unten.)

- Simple sentences consist of a main clause only.
- Complex sentences consist of a main clause and one or more sub-clauses.
- Sub-clauses begin with a conjunction (*when, that, even after, because, before ...*).
- Sub-clauses can stand before or after a main clause, or they can be embedded in a main clause.

Sieh dir den unvollständigen Merksatz und den Hinweis darüber an. Vervollständige dann den Merksatz und übertrage ihn in dein Übungsheft.

- Einfache ______________ bestehen nur aus einem _________________.
- Satzgefüge bestehen aus einem Hauptsatz und _________________ oder mehreren _________________________.
- Nebensätze __________________ mit einer Konjunktion (*when, that ...*).
- Nebensätze können ...
  - vor einem _______________________ stehen (_______________ *Greece was conquered by the Romans about 200 BC, the games took place every four years.*)
  - _______________ einem Hauptsatz stehen: (*But we know* _________ *such games took place more than 3000 years ago.*)
  - ________ einen Hauptsatz eingebettet sein: *The first documents* __________ *exist of the games at Olymia near Athens are from AD 776.*

For more about conjunctions and commas in complex sentences, see *13 Conjunctions.*

simple sentence: The games ...these contests. sub-clauses: 1. that such games ...years ago; 2. that exist ... near Athens; 3. even after Greece ... about 200 BC; 4. because he thought; 5. that they were 'unchristian'; 6. before the first ... took place

44 tenses (1): talking about the past

Zeiten (1): über die Vergangenheit sprechen

Lies die Überschrift und den Text und finde heraus, was zum Aussterben der Dinosaurier geführt haben könnte.
Finde dann die englischen Entsprechungen für 'über Millionen von Jahren entwickelten sich einige von ... zu ...', 'ein kleines Gehirn', 'sie töteten ihre Beute mit ihren mächtigen Klauen', 'vor ungefähr 65 Millionen Jahren starben die Dinosaurier aus', 'möglicherweise fand ein Klimawechsel statt', 'die Dinosaurier haben das nicht überlebt' und 'Oder sind sie aus anderen Gründen ausgestorben?'

the simple past

You use the simple past to talk about situations, events and actions that happened in the past and are over.

Dinosaurs first **appeared** about 245 million years ago. Over millions of years some developed from primitive reptiles into large and dangerous animals which attacked other animals.

Tyrannosaurus Rex **had** only a very small brain, but he was very dangerous. Raptors were much cleverer and faster. They hunted in groups and killed their prey with powerful claws.

About 65 million years ago dinosaurs became extinct. It's possible the earth's climate **changed** and plants died.
As many dinosaurs ate plants, this led first to the death of plant-eating, then to the death of meat-eating dinosaurs.

They ruled the Earth for 150 million years

One theory says that a huge asteroid collided with Earth and exploded. The dust from the explosion hid the sun for many years and the temperature fell. Dinosaurs didn't survive this.

These are some ideas, but no one really knows. Did dinosaurs really die out this way? Or did they become extinct for other reasons?

Hier hast du zwei Listen. Finde im Text die *simple past* Formen zu den Infinitiven und markiere sie. Übertrage die Listen in dein Übungsheft und ergänze sie.

Check the pronunciation of simple past endings:
appeared, killed [d]
developed, walked [t]
hunted, collided [ɪd]

regular verbs

infinitive	simple past
appear	appeared
develop	...
attack	...
hunt	...
kill	...
change	changed
die	...
collide	...
explode	...

irregular verbs

infinitive	simple past
have	had
be	...
become	...
eat	...
lead	...
hide	...
fall	...

HINT

- Regular verbs add *-ed* or *-d* at the end of the infinitive: *talk → talked; rule → ruled.*
- You must learn the simple past form of irregular verbs.
- Simple past forms are the same for all persons: *I walked, she walked, they walked.*
  Exception:
  be → I, she, he, it was,
  you, we, they were

Sieh dir den unvollständigen Merksatz und alle Hinweise auf dieser Seite an.
Vervollständige dann den Merksatz und übertrage ihn in dein Übungsheft.

- Man verwendet das ________________, um über ______________, Ereignisse und Handlungen zu ____________, die in der __________________ passierten und abgeschlossen sind.
- Die *simple past*-Form der regelmäßigen ____________ wird gebildet, indem man ______ oder ______ an den ______________ anhängt.
- ________________ Verben haben eine eigene *simple past*-__________, die man ______________ muss.
- Die Form des *simple past* ist für __________Personen ___________.
- Eine Ausnahme ist das Verb _____; es hat die Formen ______ und _______.

The situation and/or different adverbials tell you when something happened. For a list of adverbials see p.10.

- For information about negative statements, see pages 48-49.
- For information about questions, see pages 66-67.
- For more information about the simple past, see entries for *be, can, do, have, have to, may, modals* and *must.*

45 tenses (2): from the past to the present

Zeiten (2): von der Vergangenheit bis zur Gegenwart

1. spot the difference

a. Dinosaurs lived on Earth for 180 million years. ❒
b. They have been extinct for about 65 million years. ❒
c. Humans have lived on Earth for 4 million years. ❒
d. Neanderthals lived in Europe and parts of Asia for 200,000 years. ❒

1 the span of time finished in the past
2 the span of time reaches from the past to the present

Sieh dir die Sätze, das Bild und die Anmerkungen 1 und 2 an. Entscheide, was für jeden Satz zutrifft und trage die richtige Zahl in die Kästchen ein. (Die Lösung steht unter dem Hinweis.)

HINT
- When a span of time finished in the past, you use the simple past.
- When a span of time reaches from the past to the present, you use the present perfect.

a1, b2, c2, d1

- Ist eine Zeitspanne in der ____________________ abgeschlossen, verwendet man das ____________.
- Wenn eine Zeitspanne von der Vergangenheit bis zur ____________________ reicht, verwendet man das ____________________.

Finde die englischen Entsprechungen für '180 Millionen Jahre lang' und 'seit vier Millionen Jahren'.
Ergänze nun diesen Merksatz. Die Verbformen in den Sätzen oben und der Hinweis helfen dir dabei.
Übertrage den Merksatz mit je einem Beispielsatz in dein Übungsheft.

You use the present perfect when it is unimportant or when you do not know when something happened.

2. more about the present perfect

Rodolfo Coria, a paleontologist from Patagonia, Argentina

Rodolfo Coria **has looked** for dinosaur fossils all over the world, but he **has found** most fossils in the part of Argentina where he was born, in Patagonia. "My colleagues and I have proved that dinosaurs lived in South America, too. We have studied the fossils and we have learned many new things about dinosaurs."

"We have found fossils here in Patagonia that are identical to dinosaur fossils in Africa. I have seen the fossils, and they are the same. I have always believed that dinosaurs lived here before South America and Africa became two different continents. Now we have shown that it's true. – This has been the most important discovery in my career so far."

"Unfortunately, we still haven't found the reason why dinosaurs became extinct. This chapter hasn't been completed yet."

Lies den Text und finde heraus, was Rodolfo Coria und seine KollegInnen bewiesen haben.

Sieh dir die beiden Listen unter dem Text an.
Finde im Text die *present perfect*-Formen zu den Infinitiven und markiere sie.
Übertrage die Tabellen in dein Übungsheft und ergänze sie.

HINT
- The present perfect is formed with *have/has* + a past participle.
- You add *-ed* or *-d* to the infinitive to form the past participle of regular verbs: *look → looked; live → lived.*
- You must learn the past participle of irregular verbs.

regular verbs

infinitive	pres. perfect
look	has looked
prove	have …
study	…
learn	…
believe	…

irregular verbs

infinitive	pres. perfect
find	has found
	…
see	…
show	…
	be …

- infinitives: *believe, see*
- simple past forms *believed, saw*
- past participles *believed, seen*

- Das ____________________ wird auch verwendet, wenn es unwichtig ist oder man nicht ______, wann etwas in der ________________ passierte.
- Das *present perfect* wird mit *have/has* + ____________________ gebildet.

Vervollständige nun diesen Merksatz. Hilfe dabei erhältst du in den beiden Hinweisen. Übertrage den Merksatz in dein Übungsheft.

- For information about negative statements, see pages 48-49.
- For information about questions, see pages 66-67.
- For more information about the present perfect, see entries for *be, do, have, have to.*

46 tenses (3): talking about the present

Zeiten (3): über Handlungen sprechen, die in der Gegenwart stattfinden

1. the present progressive

Sieh dir an, was die Reporterin und Rodolfo sagen, und finde heraus, wie sich die Landschaft verändert hat.

Finde die englischen Entsprechungen für 'er arbeitet hier', 'ich suche Fossilien', 'wir graben hier, weil ...', 'vor Millionen von Jahren', 'eine heiße trockene Wüste', 'ganz anders', 'ein riesiger See' und 'hier sehen Sie den Fußabdruck eines Dinosauriers'.

You use the present progressive to talk about activities that are happening at the moment when you speak.

An interview with Rodolfo Coria

In der Tabelle siehst du eine Liste von Infinitiven. Finde die dazugehörigen *present progressive*-Formen im Text und markiere sie. Übertrage die Tabelle in dein Übungsheft und ergänze sie.

infintive	present progressive
talk	I'm talking ...
work	He's ...
shine	... is ...
do	What ... you ...?
look for	
dig	
stand	
look at	

Check the spelling:

shine → *shining*
dig → *digging*
lie → *lying*

HINT

- The present progressive is formed with a form of *be* (*am, are, is*) and the present participle.
- You often use the short forms of *be* (*'m, 're, 's*) after personal pronouns.
- You make the present participle with the infinitive + *-ing*.

Ergänze nun diesen unvollständigen Merksatz. Die Hinweise oben und rechts helfen dir dabei. Übertrage den Merksatz in dein Übungsheft.

- Man verwendet das ____________________, um über ________________ zu sprechen, die in dem ________________ des Sprechens stattfinden.
- Das *present progressive* wird mit einer ____________ von _______ (________, ________, ________) und dem Partizip Präsens gebildet.
- Das ______________ Präsens wird mit dem ______________ + *ing* gebildet.

2. some English verbs don't have a progressive form

Sieh dir die Überschrift, den kurzen Text und den Hinweis rechts an. Übertrage dann die Liste mit *non-progressive verbs* mit zwei Beispielsätzen aus dem Text in dein Übungsheft.

I agree with Rudolfo. **I believe** we'll find many more interesting fossils in Patagonia. **Students now want** to work here. **They hope** to discover the next 'unknown species'.

HINT

If a verb has no progressive form, you use *the simple present* to talk about the present.

non-progressive verbs:
believe, know, like, hate, prefer, remember, think, understand, want, hear, smell, sound, taste, agree, promise, belong, need, hope, ...

- For information about negative statements, see pages 48-49.
- For information about questions, see pages 66-67.
- For more information about the present progressive, see entries for *do, have*.
- For more information about the simple present, see page 80.

47 tenses (4): talking about the future

Zeiten (4): Vorhersagen machen und über zukünftige Absichten sprechen

the *will*-future and the *going to*-future

You can use the *will*- or the *going to-future* to make predictions or to speak about future intentions.

'One day scientists *will* clone an extinct species.

Then somebody *is going to* clone the first human.'

In 1936 the world's last Tasmanian tiger died in a zoo in Australia. Like the kangaroo, the tiger was a marsupial. Because it was so special, scientists kept part of the tiger in a bottle with alcohol. At the time a scientist said, "One day **we will bring this tiger back** to life. In fifty or perhaps a hundred years somebody will use the material in this bottle. I don't know how they'll do it, but the Tasmanian tiger will live again. It will be a triumph for science. Sadly, it won't happen in my lifetime."

Now, decades later, scientists have decided to do it. **They are going to re-create** the Tasmanian tiger. It's going to be very expensive and it isn't going to be easy. Critics say, "When are we going to realize that this is crazy. Scientists are going to spend $20-30 million to clone a tiger. Why can't we spend the money to save animals that are in danger before they become extinct? Is this the future? Are we going to let a species die out and bring it back to life 100 years later?"

Sieh dir das Bild sowie den Text über einen ganz besonderen Tiger an und finde heraus, was sich einige Wissenschaftler vorgenommen haben.

Finde die englischen Entsprechungen für 'eine ausgestorbene Art', 'ein Beuteltier', 'zu dieser Zeit', 'eines Tages erwecken wir diesen Tiger wieder zum Leben', 'ich weiß nicht, wie sie es anstellen werden', 'es wird sehr teuer', 'wann sehen wir ein, dass ...' und 'Lassen wir eine Art aussterben ...?'

infinitive	will-future
bring back	we will bring ... back
use	somebody ...
do	...
live	...
be	...
happen	...

infinitive	going to-future
re-create	They are going to re-create ...
be	It's ...
be	...
realize	When are ...?
spend	...
let/bring	Are ...?

In den Tabellen siehst du zwei Listen mit Infinitiven. Finde im Text die Formen des *will-future* und *going to-future* und markiere sie. Übertrage die Listen in dein Übungsheft und ergänze sie.

HINT

- The *will*-future is formed with *will* + *infinitive* for all persons.
- For negative statements you use *won't* + *infinitive*.
- The *going to*-future is formed with a form of *be* (*am, are, is*) + *going to* + *infinitive*.
- You often use the short forms of *be* (*'m, 're, 's*) after personal pronouns.

- Um über die ____________________ zu sprechen, kann man das *will-future* oder das ______________-*future* verwenden.
- Das *will-future* wird mit *will* + ______________ für alle ____________________ gebildet.
- Für verneinte Sätze benutzt man ____________ + ________________.
- Das ____________________________ wird mit einer Form von *be* (*am*, ______, *is*) + ____________________ + Infinitiv gebildet. Nach ____________________ verwendet man häufig die _________________________ (*'m, 're, 's*).

Sieh dir den unvollständigen Merksatz sowie die Hinweise oben und links an. Vervollständige dann den Merksatz und übertrage ihn in dein Übungsheft.

- For more information about negative statements, see pages 48-49.
- For more information about questions, see pages 66-67.
- For more information about the will-future, see entries for *be, can, do, have, have to.*
- For more information about the going to-future, see entries for *do, have.*

Zeiten (5): über Dauerzustände und über Dinge sprechen, die regelmäßig stattfinden

Sieh dir das Bild und den Text an und finde heraus, weshalb Kabeljau eine bedrohte Fischart ist.

Finde die englischen Entsprechungen für ‘Menschen essen seit vielen Jahrhunderten Kabeljau’, ‘dieser Fisch lebt ...’, ‘er ernährt sich normalerweise ...’, ‘auch wenn man ihn nur brät oder kocht’, ‘Trawler fangen eine Menge Jungkabeljau’, ‘der Kabeljaubestand wächst nicht wie ...’ und ‘Seehunde fressen gewöhnlich ...’.

Check your pronunciation and spelling:

This fish lives in .... [-z]
It eats other fish. [-s]
It catches smaller fish. [-Iz]

In den Tabellen siehst du zwei Listen mit Infinitiven. Finde im Text die *simple present*-Formen zu den Infinitiven und markiere sie.
Übertrage die Tabellen in dein Übungsheft und ergänze sie.

Vervollständige nun diesen Merksatz. Die Hinweise auf dieser Seite helfen dir dabei.
Übertrage den Merksatz in dein Übungsheft.

These adverbs are often used with the simple present:
always, ever, frequently, generally, never, often, sometimes, usually

48 tenses (5): permanent situations

the simple present

You use the simple present to talk about permanent situations and things that happen regularly.

Cod – another species in danger?

In Europe and North America people have eaten cod for many centuries. This fish lives in the North Atlantic and the North Sea. A cod typically weighs 11 kilos and grows over a metre long. It normally catches and eats smaller fish.

Cod is popular with so many people because it always tastes good, even if you just fry it or boil it.

Unfortunately, cod could become extinct. Every year fishing trawlers with huge nets catch lots of juvenile cod. That’s why the cod population doesn’t grow as it should.

However, humans aren’t the only danger to cod. Seals usually eat 15,000 tons of cod a year.

If we don’t protect cod, it will soon be an endangered species. On the other hand, fishermen often ask, ‘What do we do if we can’t fish for cod? Does this mean we will lose our jobs?’ – One thing is certain, the price for cod will rise.

1st & 2nd person singular, all plural forms		3rd person singular (*she, he, it,* all singular nouns)	
infinitive	**simple present**	**infinitive**	**simple present**
		live	this fish lives ...
fry	you just fry ...	weigh	... weighs ...
boil	you ...	grow	a cod ...
catch	trawlers ...	catch	it ...
eat	seals ...	eat	it ...
protect	... don’t protect	taste	...
ask	...	grow	... doesn’t grow
do	What ...?	mean	Does this ...?

HINT

- You use the infinitive for the 1st and 2nd person singular (*I, you*) and for all plural forms (*we, you, they, seals, fishermen, etc.*).
- You use the infinitive + –s or –es for the 3rd person singular (*she, he, it*) and for all singular nouns (*a fish, the cod population, etc.*).

- Man verwendet das ________________, um über Dauerzustände und über __________ zu sprechen, die __________ stattfinden. Häufig werden Adverbien wie __________, __________, __________ etc. mit dem *simple present* verwendet.

- Für die 1. und ___ Person Singular (____, *you*) und alle Pluralformen (_____, *you,* ______, *seals, fishermen* etc.) verwendet man den ____________.
- Für die ___ Person Singular (______, *he,* ____) und alle Nomen im __________ (__________, ________________ etc.) verwendet man den Infinitiv + ____ oder _____ (*lives, catches*).

- For information about negative statements, see pages 48–49.
- For information about questions, see pages 66–67.
- For more information about the pronunciation and spelling of the endings *–s* and *–es*, see entries *53 nouns (l)* and *28 verbs.*

49 tenses (6): progressive forms

You make progressive forms with a form of *be* and an *–ing* form.

Zeiten (6): Verlaufsformen

Lies den Text und finde heraus, welche Auswirkungen Vulkanausbrüche haben können.

Finde die englischen Entsprechungen für 'die ganze Stadt Pompeji', 'Kinder spielten auf den Straßen', 'das O.V. überwacht den Vulkan seit 1841', 'im Augenblick beobachten sie ...', 'in den nächsten Jahren beobachten sie bestimmte Vulkane' und 'wir würden vielleicht alle für lange Zeit in einem dauernden Winter leben'.

Im Text sind zwei Verlaufsformen markiert. Finde weitere sechs und markiere sie. – Die Tabelle mit *progressive forms* links hilft dir dabei.

Dangers from inside the Earth

Mount Vesuvius erupted on August 24, AD 79. Ash from the volcano covered the whole city of Pompeii.

On that day the sun **was shining.** Children were playing in the streets. Women and men were working.

Vesuvius has erupted many times since then. No eruption has been as violent as in AD 79.

The *Osservatorio Vesuviano* **has been monitoring** the volcano since 1841. Scientists have been watching the activities inside Vesuvius carefully.

Scientists want to predict eruptions and plan to warn people.

At the moment they are watching all the world's volcanoes carefully.

They want to predict eruptions and plan to warn people.

During the coming years they will be watching certain volcanoes very carefully.

A huge eruption could send ash into the sky, which could cover the whole planet.

If this happens, we might all be living in a permanent winter for a long time.

progressive forms: *forms of be + -ing form*

the past	was/were watching
from the past to the present	have/has been watching
the present	am/are/is watching
the future	will be watching
modals	could be watching

HINT

You use progressive forms for activities and events that are ...
- happening at a certain time
- incomplete
- happening at the same time.

Sieh dir den unvollständigen Merksatz und die Hinweise auf dieser Seite an. Ergänze den Merksatz und übertrage ihn zusammen mit der Tabelle für *progressive forms* in dein Übungsheft.

- Verlaufsformen werden mit einer Form von _______ und der *-ing*-Form gebildet.
- Man verwendet ________________________________ für ...

– Handlungen und Geschehen, die zu einer ______________________ Zeit stattfinden *(At the moment scientists are watching all the world's volcanoes)*.

– Handlungen und Geschehen, die noch nicht ________________________ sind *(The Osservatorio Vesuviano has been monitoring the volcano since 1841)*.

– zwei oder mehr ___________________________, die zur _____________ Zeit stattfinden *(Children were playing in the streets. Women and men were working)*.

You make the *-ing form* with an *infinitive* + -ing. An *-ing form* in a *progressive form* is also called *present participle*.

- For information about the forms of *be*, see pages 20–23.
- For more information about the *present progressive*, see entries for *negative statements, questions, do* and *have*.

there is, there are, ...

Sieh dir die Sprechblasen an und finde heraus, mit welchem Problem man sich in diesem Büro auseinandersetzen muss.

Finde die englischen Entsprechungen für 'entschuldige, dass ich zu spät komme', 'seit sieben Uhr verkehren keine Züge mehr ...', 'auf deinem Schreibtisch liegt eine Nachricht von ...', 'es sind zwei Kunden in meinem Büro', 'ein ernstes Problem', 'es könnte heute eine Menge Beschwerden geben', 'heute Morgen' und 'morgen sind es vielleicht doppelt so viele'.

In den Sprechblasen sind zwei Stellen markiert. Finde weitere acht Beispiele für *there + form of be* und markiere sie.

In dem Hinweis rechts fehlen die Langformen. Ergänze sie mit den Formen aus der Wolke.

50 there is, there are, ...

1. finding the forms

In English you can hear and see many sentences that start with *there* + a form of *be*.

A busy day in the office

1 Sorry I'm late. There's been a crash on the underground. I had to take a taxi. **There haven't been any trains** on the Circle Line since 7 o'clock.

2 **There's a message** on your desk from Sue. And there are two clients in my office who want to meet you. When can you talk to them?

3 There might be a serious problem with our new software. There could be a lot of complaints today.

4 This morning there were fifty e-mails from different clients in my computer. There was no time to read them all.

5 There'll probably be twice as many tomorrow. There won't be much rest for you.

- These short forms are often used:
  - *there's ...* = ______ [ðəz] or [ðeəz]
  - *there's been ...* = ______ [ðəz'bɪn] or [ðəz'bi:n]
  - *there've been ...* = ______ [ðəv'bɪn] or [ðeəv'bi:n]
  - *there'll be ...* = ______ [ðəl'bɪ]
- You always use the long form *there are ...* [ðərə] or [ðərɑ:].

there is
there will be
there have been
there has been

Sieh dir nun diese Tabelle und noch einmal die Sprechblasen oben an. Ergänze die Tabelle und knobele die Formen von *there + be* heraus, die nicht in den Sprechblasen vorkommen. (Die Lösung steht unten.)

Übertrage die Tabelle zusammen mit dem Hinweis in dein Übungsheft.

	number	positive	negative
the past	4	*there was/were*	*there ______/______*
the time from the past to the present	___	*there ______/'ve been*	*there hasn't/______*
the present	___	*there ______/______*	*there isn't/______*
the future	___	*there ______*	*there ______*
modals	___	*there might/______*	*there might not be/ couldn't be*

the past: 4; there was/were, there wasn't/weren't; the time from the past to the present: 1; there's/'ve been, there hasn't/haven't been; the present: 2; there's/are, there isn't/aren't; the future: 5; there'll be, there won't be; modals: 3; there might/could be, there might not be/couldn't be

2. *there was* or *were*, *there's been* or *'ve been*, *there's* or *are*?

Lies diese E-Mails und finde heraus, worüber Jane die Adressaten informiert.

In der ersten Mail sind zwei Stellen markiert.
Finde die Formen von *be* + *noun* in den anderen beiden Mails und markiere sie.

To: Sandy Kelly (s.kelly@planetz.co.uk)

Hi Sandy
There's been a problem with the new version of our software. We have found the problem and corrected it.
There've been no other problems so far.
Kind regards, Jane

To: Rob Payne (r.payne@a1.net)

Hi Rob
There's a problem with the new version of our software. We've found and corrected it. Contact me for an upgrade. There are no other problems with the software.
Kind regards, Jane

Software problems

To: Emma Brown (e.brown@firstshop.com)

Hi Emma
Sorry I didn't e-mail you yesterday. There was a crisis in the office. There were hundreds of complaints about our new software. Luckily, we've found the problem and corrected it. Yes, I'm free at the weekend. Let's meet.
Jane

Sieh dir den unvollständigen Merksatz und die in den Mails markierten Nomen an. Vervollständige den Merksatz und übertrage ihn in dein Übungsheft.

- Man verwendet *there was, there's* __________ und ____________, wenn ein ______________ im Singular *(a problem,* _____________*)* folgt.
- Man verwendet *there* ____________, *there* _______ *been* und ______________, wenn ein Nomen im ______________ *(problems,* _________________*)* folgt.

3. a problem for you?

Vervollständige die deutschen Entsprechungen der drei englischen Sätze. (Es gibt mehrere angemessene Übertragungen.)

Weshalb, denkst du, können diese Sätze mit *there + form of be* Lernenden Probleme bereiten?

1. There was a long queue at the taxi stand.

   Am Taxistand ________________________ eine lange Menschenschlange.

2. Is there any coffee left?

   Ist noch ____________________________?

3. Are there any similar programs on the market?

   Gibt ____?

4. an exercise

Hier hast du sechs deutsche Sätze sowie englische Satzanfänge und Satzenden. Setze die englischen Entsprechungen für die deutschen Sätze zusammen. (Die Lösung steht unten.)

1. Das muss einfacher zu bewältigen sein.
2. Wir hatten eine Menge E-Mails wegen unseres Softwareproblems.
3. Stimmt etwas mit deinem Computer nicht?
4. Waren gestern irgendwelche Anrufe für mich?
5. Es war kein Kaffee mehr übrig.
6. Um 10 Uhr haben wir eine Besprechung, um über unsre Software zu sprechen.

A. Is there …	a. a meeting at 10 o'clock to discuss our software.
B. There'll be …	b. something wrong with your computer?
C. There wasn't …	c. an easier way to do this.
D. There have been …	d. any phone calls for me yesterday?
E. There must be …	e. a lot of e-mails about our software problem.
F. Were there …	f. any coffee left.

1 E c; 2 D e; 3 A b; 4 F d; 5 C f; 6 B a

51 this/these – that/those

Demonstrativpronomen: *this/these* – *that/those*

1. singular and plural

Lies diese Texte und finde heraus, welche Biolebensmittel dieser Laden verkauft.

Finde die englischen Entsprechungen für 'diese Milch ist …', 'und das ist …', 'ich mag diesen (Käse) am liebsten', 'das sind …', 'das ganze Gemüse verkauft sich sehr gut', 'diese Biosäfte', 'die Brötchen dort sind …', 'eine hiesige Bäckerei', 'die auf dem unteren Regal(brett) dort sind …' und 'wir kaufen das (Brot) dort bei …'.

Im Text sind fünf Stellen markiert. Finde weitere Beispiele für *this/these* und *that/those* und markiere sie.

This/these 'point' to people and things near the speaker.
That/those 'point' to people and things further away from the speaker.

A new job for Becky

Here in **this part of the shop** we have our organic food. This milk is from Higher Farm. And **this is** our best-selling cheese. I like **this** best. It's from a small farm not far from here. It's very good.

These are the products from River Farm. These eggs and all these vegetables sell very well. We also buy these organic juices from River Farm. These are very popular with our customers.

All those products are organic, too. Those rolls are from a local bakery. Our customers really like those. We only have a few of those left today. Those on the lower shelf are more expensive, so we don't sell so many.

That's our bread section. That bread on the top shelf is fresh every day. We get that bread on the next shelf twice a week. We buy that from a bakery in Cornwall.

HINT

- You use *this, that* for the singular.
- You use *these, those* for the plural.

Sieh dir diese Tabelle an und finde die Sätze oben im Text.
Übertrage die Tabelle in dein Übungsheft und ergänze sie.

this
This … our best-selling cheese.
… milk … from Higher farm.
I like … best.

these
These … very popular.
… eggs … very well.

that
That … our bread section.
… bread on the top shelf … fresh.
We buy … from a bakery in Cornwall.

those
… on the lower shelf … more expensive.
All … products … organic.

Lies den unvollständigen Merksatz und die Hinweise auf dieser Seite. Sieh dir auch die im Text markierten Stellen an. Ergänze den Merksatz und übertrage ihn in dein Übungsheft.

- Man verwendet *this/*__________ für Personen und __________, die __________ beim Sprechenden sind.
- Man verwendet ________/*those* für __________ und Dinge, die weiter weg vom ________________ sind.
- *This* und ________ werden für den Singular, _________ und *those* für den______________ benutzt.

2. a problem for you?

Übertrage diese Sätze in dein Übungsheft und und füge die deutschen Entsprechungen hinzu. Weshalb, denkst du, haben Lernende häufig Probleme mit *this/these* und *that/those*?

1. This is my yogurt.
   And these are your yogurts.
2. This bag is very expensive.
   These bags are even more expensive.
3. Look at those flowers.
   That one is beautiful.
   Those are beautiful, too.

52 the time

In English you can say the time in two different ways.

die Uhrzeit

1. What you may hear ... and what it means

Sieh dir die zwölf Uhrzeiten, die Hinweise und die Uhren an.

Finde die englischen Entsprechungen für ‘fünf nach acht/acht Uhr fünf’, ‘fünf vor halb neun’, ‘halb neun’, ‘fünf nach halb neun’ und ‘Viertel vor neun’.

Ordne die ‘gehörten’ Uhrzeiten den entsprechenden Uhren zu, indem du sie verbindest. Für drei der Uhren musst du je zwei Verbindungslinien ziehen.
(Die Lösung steht unten.)

a 08:07
b 08:37
c 08:15
d 08:05
e 08:00
f 08:30
g 08:25
h 08:35
i 08:45

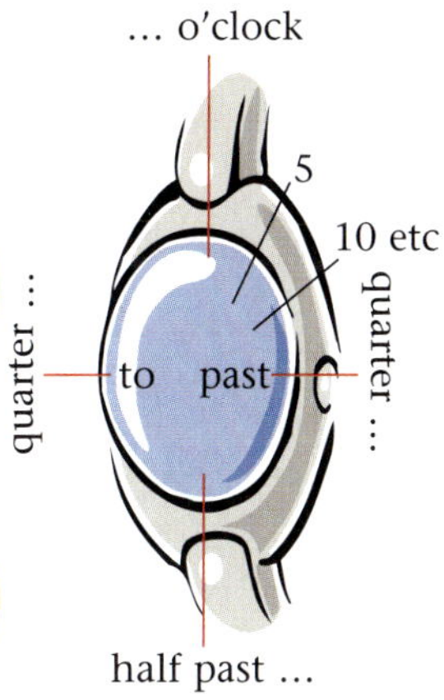

1 ... quarter to nine.
2 ... quarter past eight.
3 ... twenty-five to nine.
4 ... eight thirty-seven.
5 ... five past eight.
6 ... eight o'clock.
7 ... twenty-three minutes to nine.
8 ... eight oh seven.
9 ... seven minutes past eight.
10 ... half past eight.
11 ... twenty-five past eight.
12 ... eight oh five.

HINT

- You only use *‘... o'clock’* with full hours: ‘one o'clock, two o'clock, ...’.
- You use *‘past’* for the 30 minutes after a full hour: ‘ten past one, twenty past two, ...’.
- You use *‘to’* for the minutes before the next full hour: ‘twenty to three, ten to four, ...’.
- You use *‘minutes’* for all numbers that can't be divided by five: ‘six minutes past five, sixteen minutes to six, ...’.

2. How well can you tell the time?

	the ‘difficult’ way	the ‘easy’ way
10.03	*three minutes past ten*	*ten oh three*
11.05	*... past eleven*	*eleven ... five*
12.15	*quarter ...*	...
01.20	...	...
02.26	*twenty-six minutes ...*	...
03.30	...	...
04.33	*... to five*	...
05.45	...	...
06.47	...	...
09.00	*nine o'clock*	

HINT

If the time of day is not clear from the situation, you can say ...
six a.m. [eɪ'em] or
six o'clock in the morning
two p.m. or
two o'clock in the afternoon
six p.m. or
six o'clock in the evening
ten p.m. or
ten o'clock at night

Sieh dir die beiden Hinweise und die unvollständige Tabelle an. Übertrage die Tabelle in dein Übungsheft und ergänze sie. (Markiere vom Deutschen abweichende Bezeichnungen.) Füge die Informationen aus den Hinweisen und die *phrases* unten hinzu.

3. Some phrases to talk about the time

Useful phrases

Excuse me, can you tell me the time, please?
What's the time?
What time is it?

It's about quarter past
... It must be almost ...
I think it's just after ...
I'll be there about four.

My watch is slow.
My watch is fast.

Timetables and programmes often use the 24-hour-clock: 17.15, 20.42 ...

1i, 2c, 3h, 4b, 5d, 6e, 7b, 8a, 9a, 10f, 11g, 12d

53 verbs

Most verbs tell you what someone does.
Some tell you what happens.
Some tell you what people are or have.

Verben

Sieh dir das Bild und den Text an und finde heraus, wie unterschiedlich Menschen beim Denken ihr Gehirn benutzen.

Finde die englischen Entsprechungen für 'auf unterschiedliche Art und Weise', 'einer hört …, ein anderer sieht …', 'die Wörter erscheinen als …', 'einige Menschen entwickeln Gedanken ohne …', 'er stellte sich … vor', 'ein Lichtstrahl', 'mit Lichtgeschwindigkeit' und 'diese Vorstellung brachte ihn später auf seine … Relativitätstheorie'.

1. identifying verbs

Many people **think** in words. They **do** it in different ways. One person 'hears' the words in the brain, another person 'sees' them. For some people, the words appear as black letters. For others they come in different colours.

Many people have their thoughts in pictures. However, most people use a combination of words and pictures.

Some people form ideas without words or pictures.

We know that Albert Einstein often thought in pictures. One day, as a teenager, he imagined the following scene. He sat on a beam of light and he travelled through space at the speed of light. This idea later led him to his famous theory of relativity.

Im Text sind zwei Verben markiert. Finde weitere 13 Verben und markiere sie. (Die Lösung steht unten.)

2. some forms of a verb

Sieh dir diese Tabelle, den Hinweis darunter und den Tipp zur Schreibung an. Übertrage die Tabelle in dein Übungsheft und vervollständige sie mit den restlichen Verben aus dem Text.

Markiere die unregelmäßigen *simple past*-Formen und die dazugehörigen Infinitive in deiner Tabelle.

infinitive/ basic form	3rd pers. sing. simple present	simple past
think	…	thought
do	does	…
…	hears	…
…	…	saw
…	…	took
…	…	appeared

Note these spellings:
imagine → imagined
travel → travelled
watch → watches
cry → cries

HINT

- In a dictionary you find the infinitive/basic form and the basic meaning of the verb.
- You add *-s* or *-es* to the infinitive to form the 3rd person singular. The rules are similar to the plurals of nouns (see pages 50-51).
- English has regular verbs and irregular verbs. Most regular verbs form their simple past with *-ed*: *appear – appeared*. Some add *-d*: *use – used;* a few double the consonant: *stop – stopped, prefer – preferred*. Irregular verbs have an irregular simple past form: *do – did, hear – heard*. Learn them!
- Don't forget the *-y* rule: *fly – flies, try – tried*. (But: *play – plays, enjoy – enjoyed.*)

Sieh dir nun den unvollständigen Merksatz und noch einmal alle Hinweise auf der Seite an. Ergänze den Merksatz und übertrage ihn in dein Übungsheft.

- Die meisten ________________ drücken aus, was jemand ____________. ________________ Verben sagen aus, was geschieht; andere, was Menschen sind oder ________________.
- Es gibt ____________________ und unregelmäßige ________________.

  Die meisten regelmäßigen __________ bilden die *simple past*-Form mit _____.

  Unregelmäßige ____________________-Formen muss man auswendig lernen.

hears, sees, appear, come, have, use, form, know, thought, imagined, sat, travelled, led

3. main verbs and auxiliary verbs

Lies die Texte in den Sprechblasen und finde heraus, welche Träume und Albträume diese Menschen haben.

Finde die englischen Entsprechungen für 'die Bremsen funktionieren nicht', 'ich bin mir nicht komisch vorgekommen', '(sie) untersucht seit vielen Jahren Träume' und 'manchmal verfolgt mich ein Monster'.

I often **have** the same dream: I'**m sitting** in a car and I'm driving towards a lake. I know I **must stop** the car, but the brakes **don't work.**

Last night I dreamt that I was flying. I flew over the town and everybody looked at me. But it didn't seem strange to me.

Dreams or nightmares?

Sandra **has been** studying dreams for many years. She must have **read** hundreds of books about them. She has written a book about dreams. I've borrowed it from her.

Sometimes a monster chases me. I think it will kill me. I can't run away. It follows me wherever I go.

The English word *verb* has two meanings in German: It is *Prädikat* (a part of a sentence) and it is *Verb* (a word class).

HINT

- Four important forms of English verbs are:
  the infinitive/basic form
  (have, sit, fly, ...)
  the simple past form
  (looked, flew, had, ...)
  the past participle
  (read, flown, borrowed...)
  the -ing form
  (sitting, flying, ...)
- For all regular verbs and for some irregular verbs the simple past and past participle are the same.

verb (part of a sentence)

auxiliary verb(s)	main verb
	have
'm (am)	sitting
...	...
	know
must	...
...	...
has been	...
...	read

Sieh dir die markierten Hilfs- und Vollverben in den Prädikaten in den Sprechblasen, die Tabelle und die beiden Hinweise an. Finde die restlichen Hilfs- und Vollverben in den Sprechblasen und markiere sie.

Übertrage die Tabelle in dein Übungsheft und ergänze sie mit den restlichen Prädikaten aus den Sprechblasen.

4. be, have, do

Be, have and *do* can be full verbs and auxiliary verbs.

HINT

- The auxiliaries *be* and *have* are used with main verbs to make tense forms:
  I was flying in my room.
  I have borrowed the book.
  She has been studying dreams ...
- The auxiliary *do* is used for questions and negative statements in the simple past and simple present:
  Do you have nightmares?
  It didn't seem strange.

Keeping a dream diary

Did you have any dreams last night?
Do you sometimes have nightmares?
Why don't you keep a dream diary?
I do it regularly. It doesn't take long.

I have an exercise book near my bed.
It has all my dreams.
I have written down lots of dreams.

Reading your old dreams can be fun.
I was reading some a few days ago.
They were very funny.
The nightmares weren't very funny at the time.

Hier hast du drei kurze Texte. Finde die englischen Entsprechungen für 'Hast du manchmal ...?', 'man braucht nicht lange', 'an meinem Bett', '... Träume lesen kann Spaß machen ' und 'zu der Zeit(, als ich sie hatte)'.

Lies nun die beiden Hinweise und markiere die Formen von *be, have* und *do* als Hilfsverben oder Vollverben unterschiedlich.

- For more information see 11 *be*, 15 *do*, 16 *have*.
- For more information about negative statements, see pages 48-49.
- For information about questions, see pages 66-67.

wollen/möchte (-est; -en)/sich etwas wünschen

54 want/would like

1. tenses and time: some forms of *want*

You can use *want* in different ways:
- want + object
- want + to + infinitive
- want + object + to + infinitive

Sieh dir die Sprechblasen an: Welches Problem scheinen die jungen Leute zu haben?

Finde die englischen Entsprechungen für 'ich wünsche mir einen Freund, der ...', 'Gefühle', 'ich möchte, dass unsere Freundschaft ewig dauert', 'er wollte schon oft, dass ich ... ansehe', 'ich möchte vielleicht nur mit ihm reden', 'gestern Abend wollte ich ... ausleihen', 'sie wollte, dass ich ... ausleihe' und 'sie will den Himmel auf Erden'.

Are women really from Venus?

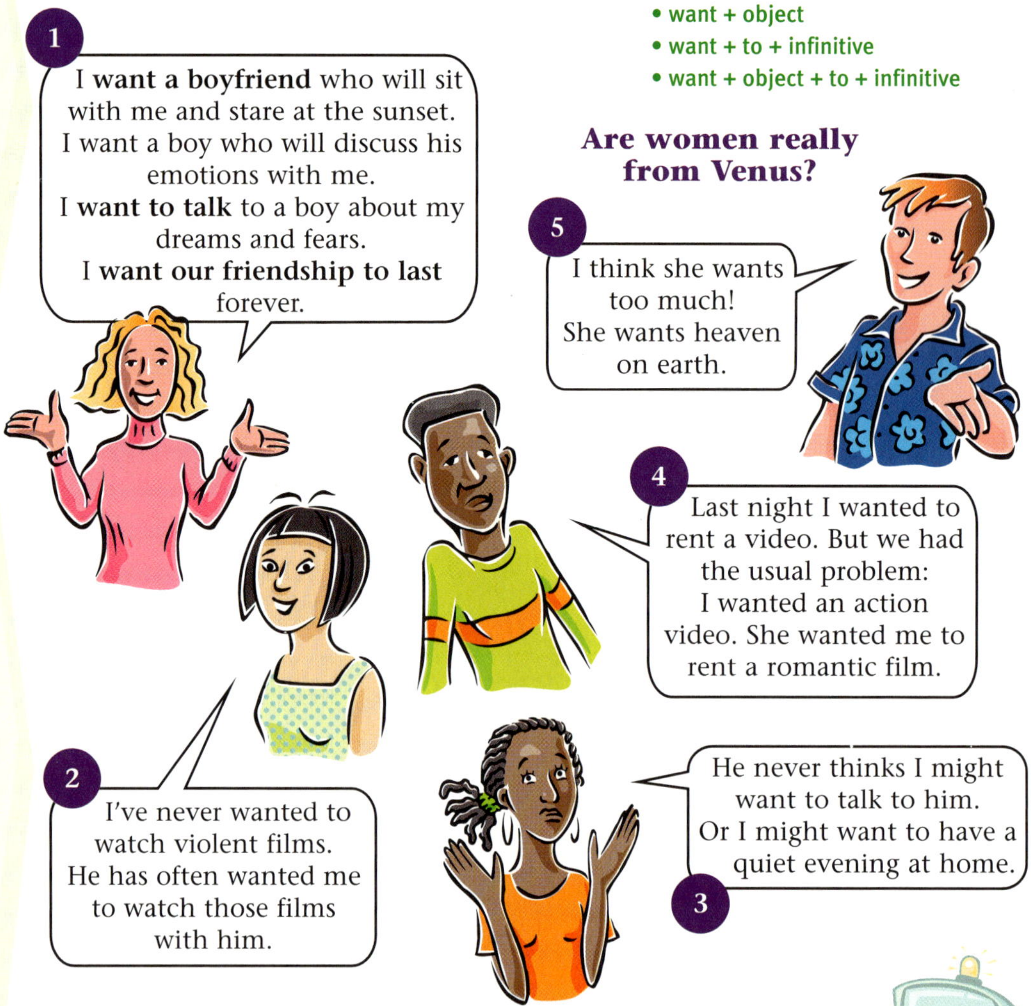

Welche Verwendungsweise, denkst du, bereitet Lernenden die meisten Probleme? Weshalb?

Sieh dir diese Tabelle, die fünf Sprechblasen und den Hinweis rechts an. Ergänze dann die Tabelle. (Die Lösung steht du unten.)

	number	forms of *want*
the past	4	*wanted*
from the past to the present	___	______ *wanted*
		has __________
the present	___/___	____________/*wants*
with modals	___	*might* ____________

HINT

- You add *-ed* to the infinitive to form the simple past or the past participle.
- You form the present perfect with *have/has* + past participle.
- For the 3rd person singular in the simple present you add *-s* to the infinitive: *He, she, it wants ....*
- There is no progressive form for *want*.

Lies den Hinweis oben und die erste Sprechblase noch einmal. Finde dann Beispiele für die drei Verwendungsweisen in den restlichen Sprechblasen und markiere sie.

2. different ways of using *want*

Lege in deinem Übungsheft drei Tabellen mit je drei Beispielen und ihren deutschen Entsprechungen an.

want + object
I *wanted* an action video.
(...)
She *wants* ...
(...)
...

want + to + infinitive
I *want to talk* ...
(...)
...

want + object + to + infinitive
She *wanted* me *to rent* ...
...

about the past: 4; about the time from the past to the present: 2, have/has wanted; about the present: 1, 5, want / wants; with modals: 3, might want

3. negative statements with *want*

Sieh dir diese Aussagen an und finde die englischen Entsprechungen für 'sie stellt oft fest, dass ...', 'sie möchten keine Jungen, die ...', '... mich seinen Freunden vorstellt', 'ich möchte, dass er mich nicht ignoriert', 'ich wollte kein ... spielen' und '..., der kleiner ist als ich'.

Are boys and girls really from different planets?

"A girl often **wants** to talk about her emotions, but she often finds that a boy doesn't want to discuss his."

"Girls **want** boys who have time for them. They don't want boys who need 6 beers before they can dance."

"I **want** my boyfriend to introduce me to his friends. I don't want him to ignore me."

"Last night I **wanted** to spend a quiet evening at home. I didn't want to play a video game or flip from one tv channel to the next."

"I wouldn't want a boy who's shorter than me. I **would want** to look up to a boy, not down on him."

Im Text sind bejahte Formen von *want* markiert. Finde die entsprechenden verneinten Formen und markiere sie.

some negative forms of *want*

the past:	____________ want	
the present:	don't ________ / ________ want	
with modals:	____________ want	

Remember!
For the present use:
- I, you, we, they → don't want.
- he, she, it → doesn't want.

Ergänze die Tabelle mit wichtigen Verneinungsformen von *want* und übertrage sie in dein Übungsheft.

4. questions with *want*

Did your boyfriend want to watch motor racing at the weekend? What did you want to watch?

Of course. I said to him: **Do you really want** to have one? They're so expensive.

He actually wants to go to a race. **Would you want** to go to a Formula 1 race? Would you want to listen to all that noise?

Why do so many men want fast cars? **Does your boyfriend want** a sports car?

Lies die Texte in diesen vier Sprechblasen und finde die englischen Entsprechungen für 'Was wolltest du sehen?', 'Möchte dein Freund einen Sportwagen?' und 'Würdest du ... gehen wollen?'

questions

about the past:	*Did your boyfriend* ______________________?
about the present:	*Do you* ______________________?
	______ *your boyfriend* ______________________?
with modals:	*Would* ______________________?

Sieh dir nun die Tabelle an und ergänze die Beispielsätze aus den Sprechblasen. Übertrage die Tabelle in dein Übungsheft.

5. polite requests and offers: *I'd like ... / Would you like ...?*

CAREFUL:

To ask politely for something, use: *'I'd like ...'*

To offer something politely, use: *'Would you like...?'* *'What would you like ...?'*

"I'm hungry."

"What ____________ you like?"

"I ____________ a sandwich, please."

"____________ you ________ a drink, too?"

"Yes, please. I'd ________ a cup of tea."

Ergänze diesen unvollständigen Dialog. Hilfe dafür findest du in dem Kasten links. (Die Lösung steht unten.) Übertrage den Kasten zusammen mit dem Dialog in dein Übungsheft.

would, would like, would … like, like

Wortarten

Sieh dir das Bild und den Text an und finde heraus, weshalb Menschen den Sternen gleichen.

Finde die englischen Entsprechungen für 'wir leben (unser Leben) behaglich ', 'nahe', 'entfernt', 'ein persönlicher Standpunkt', 'wir scheinen gut mit andern Menschen auszukommen', 'aus ganzem Herzen', 'wenn wir stur darauf beharren, dass ...' und 'Meinung'.

Lies den Hinweis zu Nomen, Verben, Adjektiven und Adverbien der Art und Weise. Sieh dir dann die Tabelle und die markierten Wörter im Text an.
Übertrage die Tabelle in dein Übungsheft und vervollständige sie mit den restlichen 20 Wörtern aus dem Text.

Lies nun diesen unvollständigen Text und sieh dir die Gruppen mit Wörtern aus den vier Wortarten an.
Vervollständige dann den Text mit diesen Wörtern. (Die Lösung steht unter dem Text.)

For more about these word classes, see entries for *nouns*, *verbs*, *adjectives* and *adverbs*.

55 word classes

If you can identify word classes, you can often understand difficult sentences better.

1. identifying major word classes

Each person **is** like a **star**. We are the **centre** of our universe and have 'planets' around us. – We live our lives **comfortably** with friends and **family**. Some are **close**, others more **distant**.

There are several billion such 'stars' on **Earth**. Each person **slowly** builds a '**universe**' that is a bit **different** from the 'universes' of other people. Everyone **lives** a little bit **differently** and **has** a **personal** point of view.

We **seem** to get on **well** with other people when we can **forget** our '**individual** universe' and try to **understand** other opinions **whole-heartedly**. **Serious** problems start when we insist **stubbornly** that our **opinion** is the only right one.

Billions of 'universes'

word classes	example words
noun	*star, ...*
verb	*is, ...*
adjective	*close, ...*
adverb of manner	*comfortably, ...*

- Nouns, verbs, adjectives and adverbs (of manner) are the major word classes.
- They carry most of the meaning of a sentence.
- In some books *word classes* are also called *parts of speech*.

2. an exercise

nouns:
sun air
centre Earth

adjectives:
well-known
flat
long
round

adverbs:
carefully
clearly
firmly

verbs:
made
move
landed
observed

For a __________ time people ______________ believed that the Earth was _________.

Around 200 BC the Greek mathematician Eratosthenes ______________ the sky, the _________ and the shadows of objects ____________________.

He ___________ an experiment and found out that the Earth was ____________.

However, people still believed that the Earth was the _____________ of the universe and didn't __________. The ____________________ Greek astronomer Ptolemy (c.100–168) believed he could prove this quite ______________: He threw different objects into the _______ and they all fell straight back to earth.

He claimed that if the ___________ had moved, the objects would have _____________ some distance behind.

long, firmly, flat; observed, sun, carefully; made, round; centre, move; well-known, clearly; air; Earth, landed

3. identifying six minor word classes

Sieh dir das Bild und den Text an und finde heraus, was vielleicht ein Schwindel gewesen sein könnte.

On July 20, 1969, over 600 million viewers sat in front of **their** TVs. **They** saw how Neil Armstrong climbed **from** Apollo 10 and walked on the moon. **During** the following years, the USA sent five more manned spacecraft to the moon. Each time two astronauts landed on the moon. – Or did they?

Was it all a hoax?

For **many** years **some** people have claimed that the Americans never landed on the moon. "**It** is **my** opinion," says one American writer, "that the landings were filmed in **our** country, in the Nevada desert. **We** didn't have the technology to land on the moon but we wanted to get there before the Russians."

These people say **that** the landscape in the films of **the** landings looks very similar to the Nevada desert. **And** in one film **an** American flag is waving, **but** there is no wind on the moon.

But if **all** this is true, how can we explain the 400 kilos of moon rock that the astronauts brought back? No scientist has ever said that **a** rock was from Earth.

Finde die englischen Entsprechungen für 'in den folgenden Jahren', 'weitere bemannte Raumschiffe', 'einige Leute haben behauptet ', 'in der Wüste Nevadas', 'wir wollten dahin kommen', 'die Landschaft in den Filmen', 'sehr ähnlich' und 'eine Fahne flattert'.

- Articles, personal pronouns, possessives, quantifiers, conjunctions and prepositions are some of the minor word classes.
- Words from the minor word classes often carry 'grammatical' meaning.
- Other minor word classes:
  reflexive pronouns (*myself, yourself...*)
  relative pronouns (*that, who, which*)
  demonstratives (*this/these; that/those*)

Sieh dir den Hinweis links, die Tabelle und die unterschiedlich markierten Wörter im Text an.

word classes	example words
articles	*a, …*
personal pronouns	*they, …*
possessives	*their, …*
quantifiers	*many, …*
conjunctions	*that, …*
prepositions	*on, …*

Übertrage dann die Tabelle in dein Übungsheft und vervollständige sie mit je zwei weiteren Beispielwörtern aus dem Text.

4. an exercise

Lies die beiden unvollständigen Texte und sieh dir dabei die Wörter darüber an. Ergänze dann die Lücken mit den Wörtern. (Die Lösung findest du unten.)

some • the • they • that • because he • a • during • in • but

________ the Renaissance (1300–1600) ________ astronomers began to study ______ sky more carefully. ________ gradually discovered ______ Ptolemy couldn't be right. ________ it took a long time to prove that ______ was wrong. ______ those days it was dangerous to say this ____________ a wrong word could cost _____ person's life.

and • of • all • a few • when he • our • him • his • the

Nicolas Copernicus (1473–1543) is often called ______ founder ______ modern astronomy. _____ discovered that the sun is the centre of ________ universe. __________ he said that ______ planets orbit the sun, only _________ people believed ________. ________ ideas were dangerous for both him ________ those people who believed them.

For more information, see entries for *articles, conjunctions, personal pronouns, possessives, prepositions* and *quantifiers*.

text 1: during, some, the, they, that, but, he, in, because, a
text 2: the, of, he, our, when, all, a few, him, his, and

Merksätze: Lösungen

page	
6	Adjektive, vor, *same, good,* nach/hinter, *seem, become, happy, fluent, successful, a good education*
7	*-er, cleaner,* langen/längeren, zwei, mehr, *more, more expensive*
7	Zweisilbige, *-y, -er, i*
8	*-est,* Superlativform, Komparativform, Superlativform, *most*
10	Zeit, Ende, Orts, Zeit, Zeit, Anfang
12	drei, Satzende, Art und Weise, Satzende, Satzende, *manner, place, time,* Satzanfang, mitten
12	*of frequency,* vor, *tell them that we will succeed,* nach/hinter, *are sometimes frightened,* nach/hinter, *will never find it*
13	Satzende, Manchmal, Satz, einem, Adverb, vor, zwei oder mehr/mehreren, nach/hinter
15	Alphabet, fünf, e, i, o, u; 21, meisten, Großbuchstaben, Anfang, Namen, Sprachen, *I.*
17	drei, Artikel, einen, *definite, the,* meisten, *the,* Laut, Vokal
18	zwei, *indefinite, a, an,* meisten Fällen, *a,* Laut, Vokal, *an*
21	Gegenwart, Zukunft, Formen, *was, were, am, are, is, will be, 'll be*
22	Fragen, *was, were,* Satzbauplan, Zukunft, Fragewort, *will, wasn't, won't be*
23	verneinten/negativen, *wasn't,* Form, *will not be*
24	Personen, verneinten/negativen, alle, *can't,* verneinte, Subjekt, Vollverb, Satzbauplan, *can/can't*
25	Zukunft, Vergangenheit, Zukunft, könnte(n)
29	*doing, do, have, doing, going,* einem, *do, do, do*
31	*have, have, you, going, have,* Verbform, einem, *does, have*
33	*has,* Gegenwart, Zukunft
35	*have to, have to, have, have to,* Verbform, einem, *does, have*

page	
36	*if, when,* Konjunktion, *If,* sicher, wenn, sobald, Zeitpunkt.
37	*progressive, be, -ing*-Form, Subjekt, Satzes, Nomen/Substantiv, Pronomen
42	*be allowed to, infinitive, were, weren't,* Gegenwart, *are, 'm not, isn't,* Zukunft, *will be, won't be*
44	Form, nie/nicht, Nach/Hinter, Infinitiv, verneinten/ negativen, nach/hinter, Fragen, vor, nach/hinter.
46	*did, accident have to happen, must, must we pay to clean the beaches, will, subject, infinitive, will we have to accept this*
47	Form, darf, *mustn't,* nicht, kann, verneinten/negativen, Vergangenheit, Gegenwart, *won't have to*
49	verneinte/negative, eine, *infinitive,* Vergangenheit, zwei, *haven't, past participle, hasn't, hasn't,* Form, *present, isn't, aren't,* Zukunft, *infinitive, won't,* Form, *infinitive, not, aren't going to,* regelmäßig, *don't, infinitive, Doesn't, doesn't,* Infinitiv
50	Nomen/Substantive, klein, *bottle, England (France, Germany), English (French, German),* Anfang
53	eine, ohne, Artikel, Singular, *is, is, is, is*
53	ohne, *quality,* mit, *the information, the quality*
54	Nomen/Substantiv, *Tom Jones's music, Mum's car,* Pluralformen, *people's opinions, children's toys,* Plural, *the singers' voices, the fans' average age*
57	*one, ones,* Nomen/Substantiv, Adjektiv, *which, one, ones,* Artikel
58	*verb,* einem, *looked,* mehreren, Vollverb, *had entered*
59	Subjekt, Objekt, einem (Eigen)namen, Pronomen, Nomen/Substantiv, Pronomen
60	Personalpronomen, vor, *He, pronouns,* nach/hinter, Präposition, *them, him, object pronouns*
61	Person, vor, *your ski suit, her purse, someone, anyone, no one,* Possessivbegleiter, *their, their goggles*

page	
62	Possessivpronomen, Nomen/Substantiv, allein, Subjekt, *Hers*, Objekt, *his*
67	Fragen, eine, *infinitive*, Vergangenheit, zwei, *has, participle, has, Has*, Form, *subject, Are, Is, using,* Zukunft, *subject, infinitive, Will, take, be, infinitive, Are, to talk to, Is, going to wait,* regelmäßig, *do, infinitive, does, Does, speak,* Infinitiv, *help, Should, leave*
69	Hilfsverb, *simple past, do*, Aussagesatz, *negatives*, verneinten/negativen, *question tag*
72	Subjekt, Relativpronomen, *contact*
75	Sätze, Hauptsatz, einem, Nebensätzen, beginnen, Hauptsatz, *Even after*, nach/hinter, *that*, in, *that*
76	*simple past*, Situationen, sprechen, Vergangenheit, Verben, *-ed, -d*, Infinitiv, Unregelmäßige, Form, lernen, alle, gleich, *be, was, were*
77	Vergangenheit, *simple past*, Gegenwart, *present perfect*

page	
77	*present perfect*, weiß, Vergangenheit, *past participle*
78	*present progressive*, Handlungen, Moment, Form, *be, am, are, is*, Partizip, Infinitiv
79	Zukunft, *going to*, Infinitiv, Personen, *won't*, Infinitiv, *going to-future, are, going to,* Personalpronomen, Kurzformen
80	*simple present*, Ereignisse, regelmäßig, *always, ever, often*, 2., *I, we, they*, Infinitiv, 3., *she, it,* Singular, *a fish, the cod population, -s, -es*
81	*be*, die Verlaufsformen, bestimmten, abgeschlossen, Handlungen und Geschehen, gleichen
83	*been, there's*, Nomen/Substantiv, *a crisis, were, 've, there are*, Plural, *complaints*
84	*these*, Dinge, nahe, *that*, Personen, Sprecher/Sprechenden, *that, these*, Plural
86	Verben, macht/tut, Einige, haben, regelmäßige, Verben, Verben, *-ed, simple past*

Index

(The numbers refer to modules.)

Index

(Die Zahlen verweisen auf die Module.)